921708 $19.95
940.54 Scorched earth
SCO

Scorched Earth

By the Editors of Time-Life Books

Alexandria, Virginia

TIME LIFE®

Time-Life Books is a division of
Time Life Inc., a wholly owned subsidiary of

The Time Inc. Book Company
Time-Life Books

PRESIDENT: Mary N. Davis

Managing Editor: Thomas H. Flaherty
Director of Editorial Resources:
Elise D. Ritter-Clough
Director of Photography and Research:
John Conrad Weiser
Editorial Board: Dale M. Brown, Roberta Conlan, Laura Foreman, Lee Hassig, Jim Hicks, Blaine Marshall, Rita Thievon Mullin, Henry Woodhead

PUBLISHER: Robert H. Smith

Associate Publisher: Ann M. Mirabito
Editorial Director: Russell B. Adams, Jr.
Marketing Director: Anne C. Everhart
Production Manager: Prudence G. Harris
Supervisor of Quality Control: James King

Editorial Operations
Production: Celia Beattie
Library: Louise D. Forstall
Computer Composition: Deborah G. Tait (Manager), Monika D. Thayer, Janet Barnes Syring, Lillian Daniels

The Cover: Two German soldiers are silhouetted against a blazing cabin during the Wehrmacht's retreat from the Soviet Union in 1943. Only after his forces suffered a series of debilitating losses beginning in the spring of that year did Hitler agree to give up ground he had wrested from the Soviets. As it withdrew west, the spent German army implemented the Führer's "scorched earth" directive, which read: "All territory which the troops are forced to yield to the enemy must be made useless to him. Every village must be burnt down and destroyed."

This volume is one of a series that chronicles the rise and eventual fall of Nazi Germany. Other books in the series include:
The SS
Fists of Steel
Storming to Power
The New Order
The Reach for Empire
Lightning War
Wolf Packs
Conquest of the Balkans
Afrikakorps
The Center of the Web
Barbarossa
War on the High Seas
The Twisted Dream
The Road to Stalingrad
The Shadow War
The Heel of the Conqueror
The Southern Front
The Apparatus of Death

The Third Reich

SERIES EDITOR: Henry Woodhead
Series Administrator: Philip Brandt George
Editorial Staff for *Scorched Earth:*
Senior Art Director: Raymond Ripper
Picture Editor: Jane Coughran
Text Editors: Paul Mathless, John Newton
Writer: Stephanie A. Lewis
Associate Editors/Research: Katya Sharpe Cooke, Trudy Pearson (Principals), Oobie Gleysteen
Assistant Editor/Research: Katherine Griffin
Assistant Art Director: Lorraine D. Rivard
Copy Coordinator: Ann Lee Bruen
Picture Coordinator: Jennifer Iker
Editorial Assistant: Alan Schager

Special Contributors: Ronald H. Bailey, Walter Guzzardi, Lydia Preston Hicks, Timothy Jacobson, Peter Pocock, Bryce Walker (text); Martha Lee Beckington, Robert L. Freeman, James M. Lynch, Danielle S. Pensley, Marilyn Murphy Terrell, Jennifer Veech (research); Roy Nanovic (index)

Correspondents: Elisabeth Kraemer-Singh (Bonn), Christine Hinze (London), Christina Lieberman (New York), Maria Vincenza Aloisi (Paris), Ann Natanson (Rome). Valuable assistance was also provided by: Pavle Svabic (Belgrade), Judy Aspinall (London), Glenn Mack, Juan Sosa, Assel Surina (Moscow), Elizabeth Brown (New York), Traudl Lessing (Vienna), Bogdan Turek, Jarek Zuk (Warsaw).

First printing. Printed in U.S.A.

Published simultaneously in Canada.
School and library distribution by Silver Burdett Company, Morristown, New Jersey 07960.

Library of Congress Cataloging in Publication Data
Scorched earth / by the editors of Time-Life Books.
p. cm. — (The Third Reich)
Includes bibliographical references and index.
ISBN 0-8094-7029-2 (trade)
ISBN 0-8094-7030-6 (lib. bdg.)
1. World War, 1939-1945—Campaigns—Eastern. I. Series.
D764.S3736 1991 91-12524
940.54'21—dc20 CIP

Other Publications:

THE NEW FACE OF WAR
HOW THINGS WORK
WINGS OF WAR
CREATIVE EVERYDAY COOKING
COLLECTOR'S LIBRARY OF THE UNKNOWN
CLASSICS OF WORLD WAR II
TIME-LIFE LIBRARY OF CURIOUS AND UNUSUAL FACTS
AMERICAN COUNTRY
VOYAGE THROUGH THE UNIVERSE
THE TIME-LIFE GARDENER'S GUIDE
MYSTERIES OF THE UNKNOWN
TIME FRAME
FIX IT YOURSELF
FITNESS, HEALTH & NUTRITION
SUCCESSFUL PARENTING
HEALTHY HOME COOKING
UNDERSTANDING COMPUTERS
LIBRARY OF NATIONS
THE ENCHANTED WORLD
THE KODAK LIBRARY OF CREATIVE PHOTOGRAPHY
GREAT MEALS IN MINUTES
THE CIVIL WAR
PLANET EARTH
COLLECTOR'S LIBRARY OF THE CIVIL WAR
THE EPIC OF FLIGHT
THE GOOD COOK
WORLD WAR II
HOME REPAIR AND IMPROVEMENT
THE OLD WEST

For information on and a full description of any of the Time-Life Books series listed above, please call 1-800-621-7026 or write:
Reader Information
Time-Life Customer Service
P.O. Box C-32068
Richmond, Virginia 23261-2068

General Consultants

Col. John R. Elting, USA (Ret.), former associate professor at West Point, has written or edited some twenty books, including *Swords around a Throne*, *The Superstrategists*, and *American Army Life*, as well as *Battles for Scandinavia* in the Time-Life Books World War II series. He was chief consultant to the Time-Life series The Civil War.

Charles V.P. von Luttichau is an associate at the U.S. Army Center for Military History in Washington, D.C., and coauthor of *Command Decision and Great Battles*. From 1937 to 1945, he served in the German air force and taught at the Air Force Academy in Berlin. After the war, he emigrated to the United States and was a historian in the office of the Chief of Military History, Department of the Army, from 1951 to 1986, when he retired.

Contents

To deprive the Soviets of shelter and supplies for the coming winter, German soldiers burn houses in a small village before

A Pall of Destruction

Smoke from burning farms and villages hung heavy over Belorussia and the Ukraine in the late summer of 1943. The German army, reeling from defeats at Stalingrad and Kursk and pressed by the Red Army at every turn, was pursuing a "scorched earth" policy, stripping and laying waste to the lands it was forced to abandon.

Large-scale destruction was not new to the eastern front; the Germans had routinely destroyed villages and executed civilians suspected of supporting Soviet partisans. The new policy, however, had a different motive: to deprive the advancing Red Army of food, shelter, communications facilities, and recruits for its ranks. "The only means of slowing down armies of this kind," one panzer general wrote, "is to totally destroy everything that can be used to feed and house them."

German troops loaded every available truck, train, and wagon with anything that might be of use to the Reich's war effort. Foodstuffs, livestock, machinery, and many thousands of labor conscripts were dispatched westward. What could not be removed was to be destroyed. In particular, the army was ordered to create a fifteen-mile-wide band of devastated territory on the east bank of the Dnieper; this artificial desert was meant to delay the onrushing enemy, giving the German forces time to regroup and consolidate their defenses behind the river.

Although the retreating soldiers could not achieve the desired total destruction, they left behind them a swath of ruin: nearly one million tons of Ukrainian grain burned; a half-million head of livestock herded west; hundreds of villages and large parts of cities put to the torch. And for the civilian population, resistance frequently meant death.

The devastation did slow enemy advances, but the advantage dwindled as the Red Army's logistics improved. The scorched earth policy, often carried out with brutality and petty vindictiveness, may even have backfired: When the Red Army swept through the shattered southern Ukraine, it swelled its ranks with 80,000 new troops from the terrorized population.

retreating westward.

Severing the Lines of Communication

Demolition experts lay explosives on a rail line, part of a campaign to destroy the Red Army's most reliable means of transport.

A blasted bridge slumps into the Dvina River at Vitebsk, one of six key Belorussian towns Hitler ordered held to the last bullet.

Burning the Russian Breadbasket

German cavalrymen set fire to stacks of grain left behind as their army fell back to the Dnieper.

Thousands of cattle shot by German soldiers rotted in fields in the Ukraine.

Flames engulf the Ukrainian capital of Kiev, which shared the fate of hundreds of communities torched by retreating Germans.

German signal troops tear down telephone cables, essential for communications along the vast eastern front.

Hauling Off the Spoils of War

A soldier turned shepherd leads Russian livestock across a bridge in October 1943.

These civilians, trudging into slavery, were among thousands of conscripted laborers sent to farms and factories in the Reich.

Countering Resistance with Terror

Stunned Kiev residents survey the bodies of civilians killed as the Germans retreated

from the city in late 1943. Thousands suffered a similar fate in cities and towns across the eastern front.

ONE

Hitler's Ill-Fated Gamble

When the spring thaws turned the Russian landscape into a sea of mud in late March of 1943, the fighting stopped, and an ominous lull settled over the eastern front. The German armies occupied positions almost identical to the ones they were holding the previous year when Adolf Hitler launched Operation Blau, the grandiose offensive that had ended in disaster at Stalingrad. Although the Soviets had driven the Germans and their Rumanian, Hungarian, and Italian allies from the Caucasus and the Don River bend, Field Marshal Erich von Manstein had miraculously turned the tables by smashing Stalin's winter offensive with a brilliant counterstroke that recaptured the Ukrainian city of Kharkov and reestablished the German line along the Mius River.

But while a map of the 1,500-mile front again showed an imposing array of German army groups stretching from the Gulf of Finland to the Black Sea, appearances belied reality. Most of the 159 German divisions were badly depleted, especially the panzer divisions, which had been worn down to an average of less than thirty battleworthy tanks apiece, most of them outmoded Panzer IIIs and Panzer IVs.

The Red Army, on the other hand, was fast becoming a juggernaut. The Soviets now outnumbered the Germans by a ratio of four to one in infantry, and the quality and quantity of their air force, artillery, and armored units had risen dramatically. The workhorse T-34 medium tank, which had first startled the Germans on their advance to Moscow in the winter of 1941, and the KV heavy tank were now rolling off assembly lines in the Ural Mountains at a rate of up to 2,000 a month. And additional support from the United States—in the form of jeeps, trucks, aircraft, and millions of tons of food—was flowing to the front through the Arctic port of Murmansk.

The easy victory that Hitler had envisioned when he invaded the Soviet Union in June of 1941 had proved a pipe dream. And now, nearly two years and 1.5 million casualties later, the Germans faced a dilemma—how to continue the struggle against an aroused and increasingly confident foe.

Field Marshal Erich von Manstein *(left)* pores over a map during Operation Citadel, Germany's massive assault on the Soviet salient centered on the city of Kursk in early July 1943. The failure of this last major offensive in the East proved devastating to the Wehrmacht.

For the first time in the war, Hitler was at a loss. The Reich was now engaged in a two-front war—and losing on both fronts. Allied strategic bombers had recently stepped up the air offensive against German cities and industrial centers, and in North Africa, Allied armies had cornered the German and Italian forces. A nervous Benito Mussolini was urging Hitler to either settle with the Soviets or erect an "east wall," a permanent fortified line across the eastern front to free up troops to confront the expected Allied invasions of southern and western Europe. Rumania's General Ion Antonescu, fearful of a vengeful Stalin, was angling for a negotiated settlement in the West in order to focus the war on the Russians. Hitler, of course, had no intention of abandoning the struggle on either front. He needed a resounding victory to restore his eroded prestige.

Beyond all this lay Hitler's abiding mistrust of his generals and gross overestimation of his own abilities. According to Manstein, "what probably did most to prejudice him was his belief that we must fight for every foot of the ground that he had won from Stalin in the winter of 1941 and that had, in his view, 'saved the German Army from a Napoleonic retreat.' " The Führer had come to think of himself as the living embodiment of military genius and determination.

In the East, however, he no longer possessed the resources to mount a general offensive, or even to maintain a prolonged static defense of the vast swath of Soviet territory still in German hands. The only solution seemed to be to launch a powerful local operation that might sap the Russian strength enough to allow the Germans to regain the initiative in certain sectors of the front. But where should such an operation take place, and how should it be conducted?

In the wake of Manstein's counteroffensive, the Soviets retained possession of a huge bulge of territory centered on the city of Kursk in the south-central portion of the front. The Kursk salient, 110 miles long, and protruding 60 miles deep into the German lines, overlapped the boundary between Field Marshal Günther Hans von Kluge's Army Group Center and Manstein's Army Group South and was sandwiched between two smaller German-held salients: one centered on Orel, 80 miles north of Kursk, the other on Kharkov, 120 miles south of Kursk. Below Kharkov, the German line extended south along the Donets and Mius rivers to the Sea of Azov.

After rejecting several proposals, Hitler settled on a plan devised by General Kurt Zeitzler, chief of the general staff of the German army. Zeitzler proposed a blow against the most obvious Soviet target—the Kursk bulge. His idea was to encircle and annihilate the Soviet forces occupying the salient with concentric attacks similar to the well-tried formula that brought notable earlier successes at Minsk, Bryansk, Smolensk, Uman, and

The Wehrmacht's Precarious Front

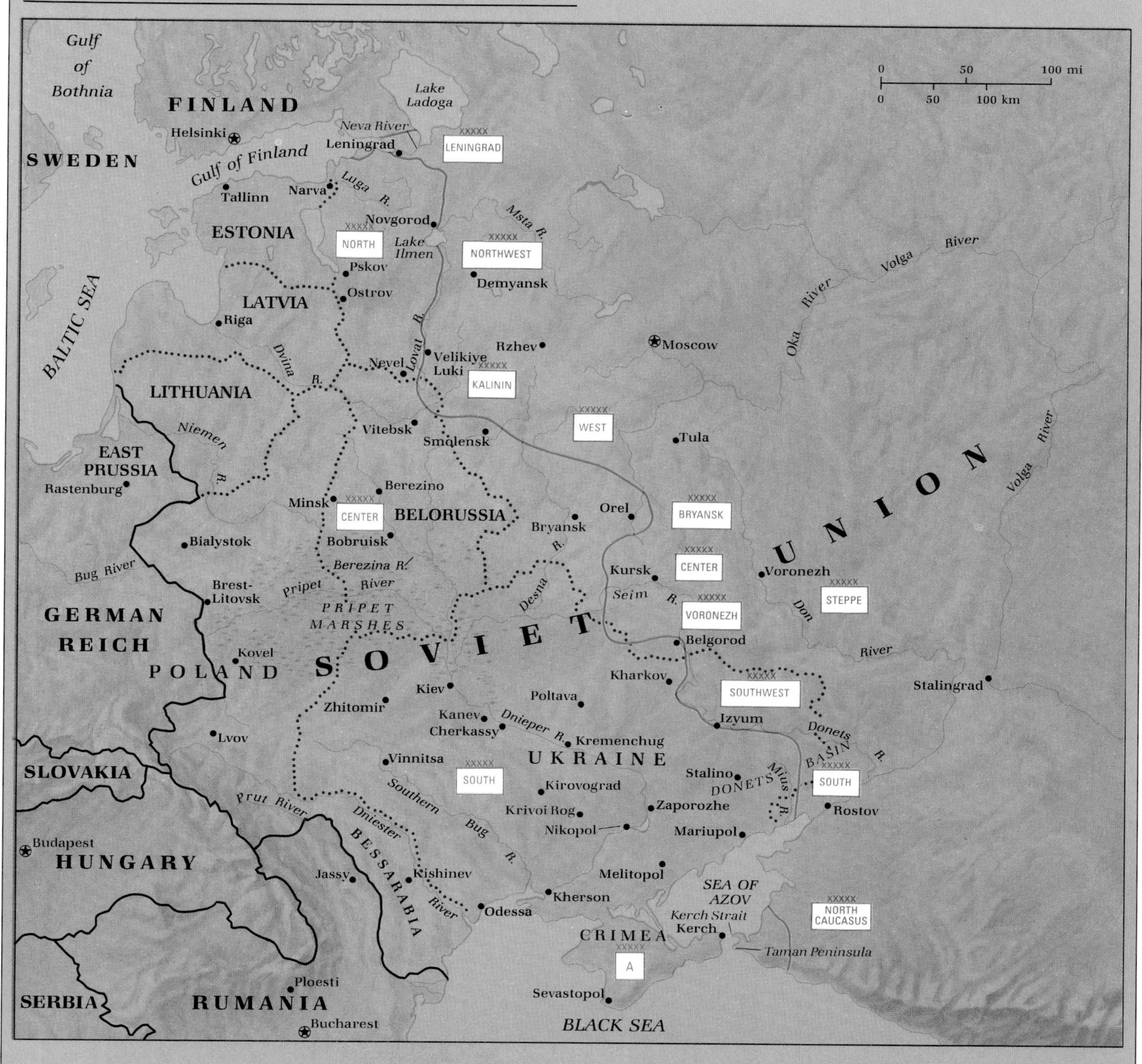

By the early summer of 1943, the front in the East had stabilized roughly where it had been a year earlier, along a 1,500-mile-long line running from the Gulf of Finland to the Black Sea. In the north, the Germans were still locked in a stalemated siege at Leningrad. To the south, following the catastrophe at Stalingrad, the Germans had been pushed out of the Caucasus and the Don River bend. But the forces of Field Marshal Erich von Manstein had counterattacked during the winter, recaptured the city of Kharkov in the Ukraine, and reestablished the German line along the Donets and Mius rivers. Manstein's counterblow had left a bulge in the line centered on the city of Kursk. In the planning of a summer offensive, Hitler set his sights on the Kursk salient, which he intended to eliminate with a massive pincers attack. It was destined to be the last major German offensive in the East.

Kiev. He would concentrate all available armor in the jaws of powerful pincers. General Walther Model's Ninth Army of Kluge's Army Group Center would attack southward out of the Orel salient, while General Hermann Hoth's Fourth Panzer Army and General Werner Kempf's provisional army of Manstein's Army Group South attacked northward out of the Belgorod salient. The jaws would snap shut on the high ground east of Kursk, shortening the front by some 140 miles and depriving the Soviets of a springboard for their next offensive.

But if the operation's potential payoff was great, so were its risks. To reinforce the Ninth Army and the Fourth Panzer Army for the assault, other armies on the eastern front would have to be stripped to the bone. The thinned-out lines northeast of Orel and south of Kharkov, where several Soviet tank armies hovered, would be left dangerously vulnerable. Any blow aimed at Kursk would have to be quick, fierce, and decisive.

On March 13, Hitler and Zeitzler flew to Kluge's headquarters at Minsk to meet with the field commanders. "It is important for us to take the initiative at certain sectors of the front, if possible before the Russians do," Hitler told them, "so as to be able to dictate their actions in at least one sector." The offensive, code-named *Zitadelle* (Citadel), was scheduled to begin as soon as the muddy ground dried out. Manstein and Kluge endorsed the plan—provided it took place before the Soviets had time to recoup their winter losses.

A swift victory would solve Hitler's problem. Perhaps he could then transfer forces used in Citadel to Field Marshal Georg von Küchler's Army Group North for a final drive against Leningrad in early summer. The capture of Lenin's namesake city, blockaded by the Germans since September 1941, would ensure Finland's continued fealty to the Reich, keep the Swedes neutral, and make Norway a less attractive target for an Allied invasion. Perhaps reinforcements could even be sent to the Mediterranean to prop up Mussolini.

But it was all wishful thinking. As it happened, the Soviets had warning of Operation Citadel. Preparations for an operation of Citadel's magnitude could not be concealed for long. The Russians learned of the shifting German dispositions almost as fast as they occurred through a variety of intelligence sources—captured prisoners, aerial photographs, monitored radio communications, partisan units behind the lines, and reports from Soviet agents in Europe. The British War Department also helped. The British had been intercepting top-secret messages transmitted by the German Enigma code machines. They passed along the deciphered transmissions, called Ultra, to Moscow. One Ultra report gave indisputable proof that a major offensive was in the works. On March 22, the British deci-

German Tiger I tanks fresh from the production line travel by rail to the eastern front in the spring of 1943. Hitler viewed the newly designed 63-ton vehicles as vital to the success of Operation Citadel and delayed the assault for two months as manufacturing problems were ironed out.

phered a message ordering the Luftwaffe's VIII Air Corps to Kharkov to support a ground movement scheduled to begin as early as late April.

Thus forewarned, General Georgy Zhukov, the Soviet deputy supreme commander, developed the strategy that would shape the fighting. The Russians would not try to beat the Germans to the punch. Instead, they would shatter the assault formations with a vigorous defense, then launch a massive attack of their own. "I consider it pointless for our forces to go over to the offensive in the near future," he told Stalin. "It would be better for us to wear out the enemy on our defense, to smash his tanks, and then, by introducing fresh reserves and going over to the offensive, to beat the main enemy force once and for all."

The Central Front army commanded by General Konstantin Rokossovsky occupied the northern half of the Kursk bulge, the Voronezh Front of

General Nikolay Vatutin the southern half. All of the villages and hamlets within the bulge were evacuated, and with Stalin's approval, Zhukov ordered Rokossovsky and Vatutin to prepare deeply echeloned defenses all across the rolling steppes, focusing on the expected attack routes south of Orel and north of Belgorod. The complex antitank defenses, which were organized down to the company level and designed to funnel the attacking panzers into a killing zone of enfilade fire, formed the backbone of the

system. "All our soldiers became engineers," one Russian officer recalled. "We dug hundreds of kilometers of trench lines and communications trenches; built cover for tanks, guns, motor vehicles, and horses; and roofed dugouts for the soldiers, which even a 150-mm shell could not damage. Everything was adapted to the terrain."

Tanks from General Hermann Hoth's Fourth Panzer Army leave wakes of crushed grass as they roll north from Belgorod toward the city of Kursk.

In addition, Zhukov instructed Rokossovsky and Vatutin to keep several armored corps in reserve. These forces would be backed up by yet another armored reserve, the powerful Steppe Military District (later called the Steppe Front), led by General Ivan Konev and deployed along the far eastern portion of the Kursk salient.

On April 15, one week after Zhukov submitted his plan to Stalin, Hitler issued Operation Order no. 6, making Citadel the "first of this year's offensives." He told his commanders: "The victory at Kursk must be a beacon seen around the world." The offensive was scheduled to begin on six days' notice any time after April 28. The Führer exhorted his commanders to maintain complete secrecy and on no account to allow the Russians to force a postponement. Yet he himself would delay Citadel over and over again, turning what was originally conceived as a reasoned and logical operation into a wild gamble.

Order no. 6 had been in the hands of the field commanders only a few days before General Walther Model grew reluctant. He complained that his Ninth Army was still 26,000 men understrength and lacked sufficient numbers of tanks, heavy artillery, rocket launchers, and self-propelled assault guns to punch through Zhukov's fortifications, which had been revealed by Luftwaffe reconnaissance photos to already be twelve miles deep in places. Model was also alarmed by reports that the Soviets' new 76.2-mm antitank gun could penetrate the armor of his Panzer IV tanks. Would it not be wiser, he asked Hitler, to prepare a defensive line along the Desna River and wait for the Soviets to attack first?

As one of the few staunch Nazis among the army's ranking officers, Model enjoyed Hitler's special trust. The Ninth Army commander's comments worried the Führer, and on April 28, with Citadel on temporary hold because of rainy weather, he summoned Model to Munich.

After listening to Model's report and examining aerial photographs of the growing Soviet defenses, a concerned Hitler canceled Citadel's timetable and ordered his eastern-front generals to the Bavarian capital to rethink the attack. The conference convened on May 4. The participants included Zeitzler, Manstein, Kluge, General Hans Jeschonnek, chief of the general staff of the Luftwaffe, General Alfred Jodl, chief of the operations staff for the armed forces high command, Minister of Armaments Albert Speer, and the renowned tank expert, General Heinz Guderian, recently appointed by

On the outskirts of Kursk, Red Army soldiers dig trenches and cover an underground communications center with sod. While Hitler vacillated, the Soviets strengthened their defenses and, with the help of 300,000 civilians, improved supply routes by repairing more than 250 bridges and 1,800 miles of roads and railroad tracks.

Soviet tank crews inspect their T-34s in preparation for the battle for Kursk. To train their troops to fight the larger and much-feared German tanks, Soviet commanders employed the T-34s in mock combat.

Hitler to serve in the new position of inspector general of armored troops.

Charged with reinvigorating the panzer forces of the army, Guderian was working closely with Speer overseeing the production of a new generation of German armor. Hitler was counting on these so-called superweapons to overcome the Soviets' numerical superiority. They included the Tiger, a heavily armored, 63-ton tank that was designed to outperform the Soviet KV heavy tank and already in service in small numbers; the 49.3-ton Panther, Germany's answer to the Red Army's redoubtable T-34 medium tank; and a 74.8-ton tank destroyer, armed with an 88-mm gun. The tank destroyer, originally called Elephant, had its name changed to Ferdinand to honor its designer, Ferdinand Porsche, the civilian automobile manufacturer and creator of the Volkswagen.

Hitler opened the conference with a short speech outlining the situation on the eastern front. Then, he launched into a summary of Citadel and Model's arguments against it, emphasizing his fear that the attacks would fail to break through the Russian defenses fast enough to complete an encirclement. "The manner in which Hitler expressed these opinions of Model's made it plain that he was impressed by them," Guderian recalled, "and that he had by no means decided to order an attack along the lines proposed by Zeitzler."

But the generals themselves could not reach a consensus on the best course of action. Field Marshal von Kluge, perhaps angry that his subordinate had bypassed him and reported directly to the Führer, suggested that Model had exaggerated the weaknesses of the Ninth Army. Kluge pressed for an attack as soon as possible, claiming further delay would only allow the enemy more time to strengthen its defenses. Manstein, Zeitzler, and Jeschonnek agreed.

Guderian, on the other hand, bluntly called the offensive "pointless" and urged that it be abandoned altogether. Even if Citadel succeeded, he argued, the resulting losses of armor would do irreparable harm to his plans for reequipping the panzer divisions for the struggles that lay ahead. "We ought to be devoting our new tank production to the western front," he said, "so as to have mobile reserves available for use against the Allied landing, which could be expected with certainty to take place in 1944."

Speer and Jodl supported Guderian. The armaments minister pointed out that the new weapons still had various technical defects and that not enough of them had been manufactured yet. Shortages of raw materials were playing havoc with production schedules. The Henschel tank plant, for example, was turning out only twenty-five Tigers a month. Panther production was even slower, at a rate of only twelve tanks per month.

Hitler listened to all the arguments but refused to make a decision. A few days after the generals returned to their posts, the army high command (OKH) delivered an announcement: The Führer had postponed Citadel until June 12 to allow extra time for the weapons factories to meet their production quotas. In the meantime, the Panzer IVs and self-propelled assault guns were to be equipped with special protective aprons.

No sooner had the news reached the field than another commander voiced his displeasure. General Werner Kempf complained that the delay would cause morale problems for his anxiously waiting assault troops.

Guderian also tried again to persuade Hitler to change his mind. Back in Berlin on May 10, the panzer expert was at the Reich Chancellery for a meeting about the new Panthers. Afterward, he seized the moment to grasp the Führer by the hand and beg him to reconsider Citadel.

"Why do you want to attack at all in the East this year?" he asked.

Before Hitler could respond to the question, Field Marshal Wilhelm Keitel, chief of the armed forces high command, interrupted: "We must attack for political reasons."

"How many people do you think even know where Kursk is?" Guderian retorted. "It is a matter of profound indifference to the world whether we hold Kursk or not. I repeat my question."

"You are quite right," Hitler responded. "Whenever I think of this attack, my stomach begins to churn."

But despite his misgivings, Hitler remained inflexible. He was determined to reinforce the panzer divisions with the new armor and proceed with the attack—even though the conditions that had prompted Zeitzler to suggest the offensive back in March had long since changed. Instead of a surprise blow against a weary and off-balance enemy, Operation Citadel, it was becoming increasingly obvious, would be a head-on trial of strength.

Three days after the disquieting exchange with Guderian, Hitler received word that the last of the 275,000 Axis troops trapped in Tunisia had surrendered to the Allies. This catastrophe had been unfolding for months, but only now did the Führer face up to the reality. Surely an Allied invasion of Italy or the Balkans would follow soon. Although Kluge and Manstein both insisted that to attack the Kursk salient at any time after mid-June would be folly, Hitler ignored his army group commanders' advice and postponed Citadel until late June to allow time for the Allied armies to reveal their next target. When he became convinced that it would be Greece, he ordered that the crack 1st Panzer Division be rushed to the Peloponnesus from France, over Guderian's fuming objections.

As the frustrating weeks wore on, the generals agonized over the dangers that the delay was creating. Hoth complained that chances of victory were lessening with each passing day, while Model grimly predicted that the coming battle would be a "collision between armies at the peak of readiness." Fearful of Citadel's risks and of the growing uncertainties facing the Wehrmacht in the West, the operations staff of Hitler's armed forces high command came out squarely against the attack. But Zeitzler and the general staff of his army high command continued to support it, arguing that to abandon Citadel now would only put the Army in a worse predicament. Meanwhile, Hitler still had not decided on a starting date.

The Panther's Troubled Debut

Designed in a hurry to contend with the formidable Soviet T-34 tank, the German Panther was rushed to the battlefield at Kursk in July 1943 with high hopes and a score of teething problems. The prototype Panther was plagued by a host of mechanical difficulties, including engine fires and drive-train failures, which prompted General Heinz Guderian to plead with Hitler to delay Operation Citadel until the Panther's problems could be eliminated. But the battle commenced as planned, and the Panther's performance on the field fully justified Guderian's fears about what he called their "premature commitment." Broken-down Panthers lined the route from railheads to assembly areas, and many more of the tanks failed on the battlefield itself. Parts originally designed for use in lighter tanks collapsed under the strain of the increased weight and power of the Panthers. Mechanical failures plus battle losses on the first day of Citadel reduced the number of available Panthers in the Fourth Panzer Army sector from an original 200 to 40.

Although the Panther's problems were solved soon after Kursk, the tank was never produced in sufficient quantities to turn the tide against the Soviet onslaught.

Panzer V-D Panther

With a high-velocity 75-mm gun and steeply sloped frontal armor inspired by the rival T-34, the Panther D was a powerful addition to the Wehrmacht's armored arsenal. Its killing range was more than ten times that of the latest-model T-34s.

On June 25, Hitler finally made a decision: Citadel would begin in the predawn hours of July 5. Soon afterward, he ordered Manstein to fly to Bucharest for the alleged purpose of presenting the Rumanian leader, Ion Antonescu, with the Gold Crimea Shield on the anniversary of the capture of Sevastopol. With the Army Group South commander off on a ceremonial mission, the Führer hoped to deceive the Russians into thinking that no major attack was imminent. Before the field marshal took off on July 1, Hitler summoned him to Wolfsschanze (Wolf's Lair), his headquarters in East Prussia. There, Manstein found Kluge, Model, Hoth, and Kempf, who had been assembled by Hitler for a final review of the tactical plan.

It had remained remarkedly unchanged: While the dangerously weakened Second Panzer Army of General Rudolf Schmidt blocked the western edge of the bulge, Model's Ninth Army would drive southward out of the Orel salient. At the same time, Hoth's Fourth Panzer Army, its right flank screened from the Soviet reserves by Army Detachment Kempf, would strike northeastward from Belgorod. The two forces would race for Kursk and link up in a matter of days.

Invigorated and overhauled, Manstein's and Kluge's army groups now had a total of 900,000 soldiers and more than two-thirds of all the panzer and motorized infantry divisions on the eastern front, armed with 2,700 tanks and assault guns. They would be supported by 1,800 aircraft. Two years earlier, Hitler had invaded the Soviet Union with a force of comparable size. But then, the front had been 1,500 miles wide. Now, the combined fronts of Model and Hoth totaled no more than four score miles.

Arrayed against this powerful German concentration would be three Soviet army groups with more than 1.3 million soldiers, 3,300 tanks, and 20,000 artillery pieces, including 6,000 antitank guns, 900 Katyusha rocket launchers, and 2,600 aircraft. Rokossovsky's Central Front still guarded the northern sector of the bulge and Vatutin's Voronezh Front the southern, with Konev's armored and infantry reserves behind them.

During the long months of Hitler's vacillation, the Red Army had burrowed deep into the black earth, sowing hundreds of thousands of mines, turning every acre of ground into an integrated maze of camouflaged trenches, antitank ditches, dugouts, and bunkers. Every farmhouse and hilltop had been converted into a strongpoint for flamethrowers, machine guns, and mortars. Front-line defenses were now 25 miles deep, with fallback positions reaching up to 100 miles.

Hitler's clever deception had been utterly for naught. As Manstein flew back to his command post via Bucharest, the Russians were already expecting an attack to occur between July 3 and 5. How they knew Citadel's approximate starting date remains one of the war's mysteries. But it is clear that the Soviets benefited from an extraordinary espionage network that had penetrated the German high command. A secret agent, or more likely a collection of agents, code-named Werther after one of Goethe's tragic characters, conveyed the information through a spy center in Switzerland orchestrated by the Hungarian communist Alexander Rado and a German refugee named Rudolf Rössler.

The careful Russian preparations forced Manstein to begin the battle half a day ahead of schedule in the south. Weeks earlier, Vatutin had pulled his front back five or six miles to behind a ridge of hills that effectively concealed his defensive network from the German ground observers. The difficulty of distinguishing between the Soviet dummy positions and the actual ones limited the value of aerial reconnaissance photographs. Before the main attack could begin, these hills would have to be seized.

The job began under cover of darkness on the night of July 3-4, as small parties of sappers crept forward to probe for mines with long metal rods. One ten-man team dug up no less than 2,700 mines from a field leading to the town of Butovo at the foot of the hills. The Russians sent up flares and braced for the assault at dawn. But nothing happened, and the morning passed uneventfully.

The weather was hot and humid, broken only by a brief afternoon thunderstorm. Shortly after the skies cleared, at 2:50 p.m., several squadrons of Stukas from the VIII Air Corps screeched down, pulverizing the approach to the hills with 2,500 bombs. The artillery preparation followed ten minutes later, then the assault. As the panzers roared forward, the Russians answered with their own guns. "The Russian artillery plowed the earth around us," a crewman of a Tiger tank recalled. "Ivan, with his usual cunning, had held his fire in the weeks before. But now, the whole front was a girdle of flames. It seemed as if we were driving into a ring of fire. Four times our valiant 'Rosinante' shuddered under a direct hit, and we thanked the fates for the strength of our good Krupp steel."

After two hours of combat, Hoth had accomplished his mission. By nightfall, the signal corps had installed telephone linkups between the new German artillery posts occupying the captured ground, and artillery observers began directing fire on the Soviet defenses in front of them.

Manstein, who had moved his headquarters from Zaparozhe to a railroad car close behind the German lines, now had his starting line. Because of the depth of the Russian defenses, he ordered Hoth and Kempf to attack with a *Panzerkeil,* or armored wedge, maneuver, rather than follow the traditional method of leading with the infantry. Instead of being fed into the battle after an opening had developed, more than 1,000 tanks and 300 assault guns would be hurled against the enemy, with the idea of blasting through the initial fortifications, then racing to engage the Soviet reserves in the open country outside of the main Russian defensive system. The succession of wedge formations would be led by the thick-skinned Tigers, with the Panthers and Panzer IVs fanning out behind, followed by panzergrenadiers armed with automatic weapons and grenades, and finally by mortar teams riding in tracked personnel carriers.

At half past three the next morning, July 5, the German guns roared into action, firing salvo after salvo into the Soviet lines. During the next forty-five minutes, they consumed more shells than the entire German army used during the Polish and French blitzkrieg campaigns.

Manstein focused the main thrust on a thirty-mile-wide sector west of

At the beginning of the battle for Kursk on July 5, 1943, a German battery fires 150-mm field guns at Soviet troops who were dug in east of Belgorod.

Belgorod and north of the sugar-beet farming community of Tomarovka. General Otto von Knobelsdorff's XLVIII Panzer Corps, consisting of the veteran 3d and 11th Panzer and elite Grossdeutschland Panzergrenadier divisions, attacked from northwest of the town while General Paul Hausser's II SS Panzer Corps, made up of the 167th Infantry Division and the three crack Waffen-SS panzer divisions, Leibstandarte (Bodyguard) Adolf Hitler, Totenkopf (Death's Head), and Das Reich, attacked from the northeast side. Simultaneously, General Eugene Ott's LII Army Corps pushed forward on the left flank, while on the right flank, Army Detachment Kempf crossed the Donets south of Belgorod, pushing north toward Rzhavets.

Shortly after the Army Group South forces got underway, the Soviets

Operation Citadel and Its Aftermath

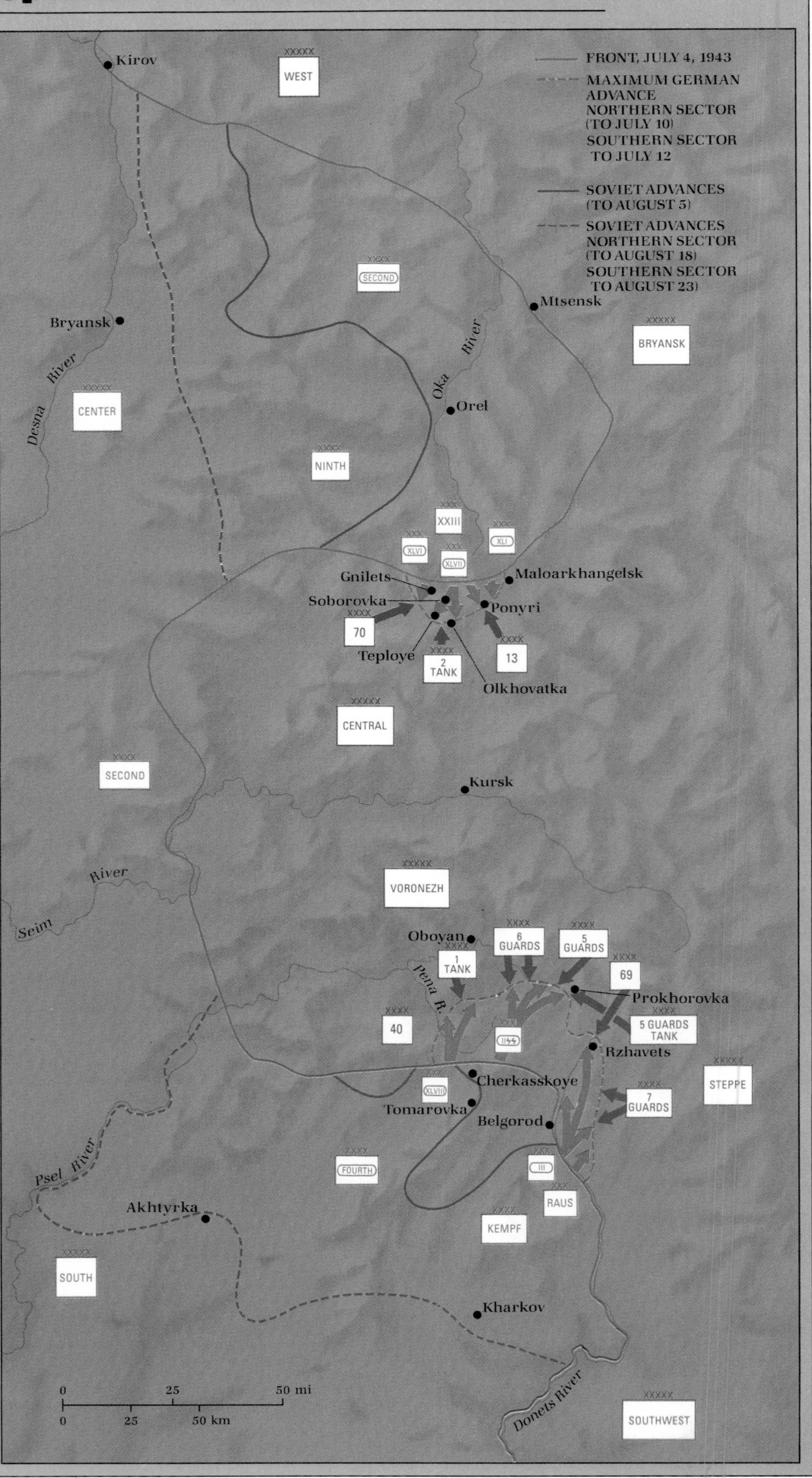

Operation Citadel, the German plan to annihilate the Soviet armies inside the Kursk salient, called for a giant pincers movement: The Fourth Panzer Army and Army Detachment Kempf of Manstein's Army Group South were to attack northward from Belgorod, while the Ninth Army of Kluge's Army Group Center attacked southward from south of Orel. But instead of linking up at Kursk as planned, both drives were blunted by fierce Soviet resistance: from the Central Front in the north, and from the Voronezh and Steppe fronts in the south. On July 13, 1943, three days after the Allies invaded Sicily, Hitler abandoned Citadel to rush reinforcements to Italy. The outcome of the fighting was still in question in the southern part of the salient, but in the north, Kluge's forces had already begun pulling back under heavy counterattack from the Bryansk and West fronts. Soon, Manstein's forces had to withdraw. By late August, the Soviets had recaptured Kharkov and were pushing inexorably westward.

launched what they hoped would be a preemptive air strike against the VIII Air Corps. Hundreds of Soviet Yaks, Lavochkin La-5s, Petlyakov Pe-2s, and the new Il 2 Sturmoviks streamed in at 10,000 feet toward the sixteen German airfields located around Belgorod and Kharkov. The Luftwaffe radar, called Freya after the Norse goddess of love and fertility, detected the Soviet formations when they were still sixty miles away, and the fighters scrambled to meet them. The Messerschmitts took a deadly toll, but not enough to knock the Soviet air force out of action.

On the ground, a torrential downpour had hit the XLVIII Panzer Corps's area, flooding the streams and turning the dry gullies into impassable swamps. The Grossdeutschland Division, mired in the muck, suffered its first setback when the Russian artillery caught it in the open. On the right, the II SS Panzer Corps also came under heavy fire from the Soviet Sixth Guards Army. But with the help of well-orchestrated air support, especially from the Stukas equipped with two 37-mm guns, the Waffen-SS divisions advanced against stiff opposition.

By nightfall on July 5, both of Hoth's corps had penetrated about five or six miles and had captured the village of Korovino, which anchored the western end of the Soviet defenses. But trouble was brewing on the right flank, south of Belgorod. Lacking the air support given the other ground units (the Luftwaffe simply did not have enough planes to be everywhere at once), Army Detachment Kempf was having difficulty getting started. Although Kempf's III Panzer Corps and Provisional Corps Raus had managed to secure a small bridgehead over the Donets, neither could push through the Russian fortifications between the river and the Belgorod-Kursk highway. And both units had suffered alarming casualties, inflicted by the Red Air Force and General Mikhail Shumilov's Seventh Guards Army.

The next day, July 6, Hoth's fortunes improved. Fighting in an artificial twilight caused by the swirling dust and smoke, the XLVIII Panzer Corps broke through the front of the Sixth Guards Army, while the II SS Panzer Corps drove back the First Tank Army. The German wedge advanced across the Belgorod-Kursk highway some twelve miles into the Russian defenses toward Prokhorovka. The Soviet army was now split in two. And on Hoth's right, Kempf's forces finally broke out of their bridgehead on the Donets and began progressing northward toward Rzhavets.

As to the objective of Hoth's main spearheads, Vatutin thought there could be no doubt. He fully expected the panzers to strike directly northward toward Oboyan and force a crossing of the Psel River, the last natural barrier before Kursk. In fact, Hoth's orders from OKH specifically instructed him to do just that. But Luftwaffe photographs had revealed that the Soviet First Tank Army of General Mikhail Katukov was blocking the way and that

General Ivan Konev's armored reserves were lurking east of the village of Prokhorovka. Hoth feared that his troops would be counterattacked by both Soviet forces as they attempted to cross the river. So the veteran panzer commander changed plans. "It is better first to dispose of the enemy who is expected at Prokhorovka," he told his commanders, "before the thrust northward toward Kursk is set in motion."

Hoth directed Hausser to take the II SS Panzer Corps northeastward to intercept Konev's reserve troops. Meanwhile, Knobelsdorff was to direct the main body of the XLVIII Panzer Corps to Oboyan. After seizing the Psel River crossing, Knobelsdorff's troops would pivot eastward to assist Hausser, while Army Detachment Kempf provided flank cover against the southernmost reaches of the Voronezh Front.

Alarmed by the German penetration north of Belgorod, the strategists of Stavka began committing the Soviet reserves to support Vatutin's Voronezh Front. General Vatutin transmitted an anxious order to his generals: "On no account must the Germans break through to Oboyan." On the evening of July 7, Nikita Khrushchev, a member of Vatutin's military council, described the situation bluntly at Katukov's First Tank Army headquarters: "Either we hold out, or the Germans take Kursk. They are staking everything on this one card. For them, it is a matter of life or death. We must see to it that they break their necks!"

Meanwhile, 100 miles away, General Model's Ninth Army, the northern jaw of the German pincers, had gotten off to a stumbling start. On July 4, before a shot was fired on the northern front, Model's rival commander, General Rokossovsky, enjoyed a bit of good luck. A Soviet patrol had surprised a German mine-clearing party, killing several soldiers and capturing a lance corporal. The prisoner informed his captors that the Germans planned an artillery bombardment at 3:30 a.m., followed by the main attack.

Should the prisoner be believed? Rokossovsky hastily consulted his superior, General Zhukov, who happened to be at Central Front headquarters. Although Red Army doctrine called for counterfire to smash enemy units while they were forming, both generals knew from bitter experience that to do so without Stalin's approval was to risk their careers. Zhukov told Rokossovsky to go ahead; he would clear it himself with the Soviet leader. At ten minutes past one in the morning, Rokossovsky opened fire on the German assembly areas and approach roads.

To the nervous commanders of the Ninth Army, the unexpected nighttime bombardment seemed to preface a Russian attack. It did not, but the shelling sufficiently disorganized Model's formations to throw off his timetable. While the artillery bombardment went off on schedule at 3:30 a.m., the ground attack was delayed by one and a half to two hours. Not until

On the first day of Operation Citadel, wounded Germans rest at a field hospital set up in an antitank ditch. Although the Germans knew they would encounter some resistance, the ferocity of the Soviet reaction was unexpected. Reported a German officer, "Nowhere has the enemy been taken by surprise. Nowhere has he been soft."

dawn did the Germans advance against the Soviet Thirteenth Army, which blocked the main route to Kursk.

Unlike Manstein, Model elected to attack first with the infantry divisions of his panzer corps. Among his six panzer divisions and one panzergrenadier division, only one, the 20th Panzer, was committed to the first wave. He planned to feed in the others after the assault troops had punched a hole through the enemy lines.

Model's immediate objective was the high ground at Olkhovatka, some ten miles deep into the salient. These hills, stretching about fifteen miles from Ponyri in the east to Molotychi in the west, stood at the middle of the Central Russian Ridge, which ran across the neck of the salient from Orel in the north to Belgorod in the south. If the Ninth Army could command them, Model would have downhill sledding to Kursk.

Shortly after 5:00 a.m., the Germans attacked along a thirty-five-mile-wide front from Maloarkhangelsk in the east to Trosna in the west. The XLVII Panzer Corps aimed the main blow along the Orel-Kursk highway and

Two Stukas swing low for a close look at Waffen-SS troops headed for Kursk *(right)*. To avoid being accidentally fired on by the Luftwaffe, a German antiartillery unit displays a swastika *(below)*.

railroad, toward the villages of Gnilets and Bobrik. The flanks of this narrow spearhead were guarded by the XLVI Panzer Corps on the west and by the XLI Panzer Corps and XXIII Infantry Corps on the east.

As the day wore on and reports filtered back from the front, a fretful theme began to recur. Although the front was moving southward, progress was exceedingly slow and costly. The toughness of the resistance confirmed all of Model's bluntly expressed fears. The Russians had no soft spots. The enemy trenches seemed endless, and they devoured the German attackers. When darkness fell, most German units were still tied up in the first defensive belt.

On July 6, Model decided to unleash more armored divisions. Checking his situation maps, he targeted the central sector of the front, north of Gnilets, where the XLVII Panzer Corps had punched a substantial hole in the Russian defenses. He committed the 2d, 9th, and 18th Panzer divisions, but still held back the 4th and the 12th and the 10th Panzergrenadier divisions for possible follow-up. Under any circumstances that Model had experienced previously, the additional panzers should have been enough to do the job. This time they were not. By nightfall, the XLVII Panzer Corps had advanced a scant six miles, and its left flank was dangerously exposed. Outside of Maloarkhangelsk, the XXIII Infantry Corps had been unable to blast through the tenacious resistance of the Soviet Thirteenth Army.

The first forty-eight hours of combat had cost the Ninth Army more than 10,000 men and approximately 200 tanks and self-propelled guns. With Rokossovsky's soldiers still dug in on both sides of the heights and his armored reserves coming from the east, Model begged Zeitzler for the immediate release of 100,000 rounds of ammunition for his armored forces. On July 8, he fed in his last armored reserve, the 4th Panzer Division. The fresh troops succeeded in pressing as far as the village of Teploye, a few miles west of Olkhovatka, but no farther. For three bloody days, the armies slugged it out over the last line of hills, in what Model described as a "rolling battle of attrition."

On the night of July 10-11, Model committed his last motorized infantry—the 10th Panzergrenadiers—to try to break the deadlock on the east side of the ridge at Ponyri, a village along the Orel-Kursk railroad. They failed. Badly battered and exhausted, the Ninth Army remained on the wrong side of the Olkhovatka hills.

The fate of Citadel now rested with Army Group South. During the previous few days, the progress of Hoth's Fourth Panzer Army had improved measurably. The 11th Panzer and Grossdeutschland divisions, the main body of the XLVIII Panzer Corps, were driving on Oboyan from either side of the Belgorod-Kursk road. By July 10, both units had reached the heights overlooking the Psel Valley and could see the towers of Oboyan in the distance. The following day, July 11, the Totenkopf Division of II SS Panzer Corps secured a bridgehead on the Psel River three miles west of Prokhorovka. Meanwhile, the Leibstandarte and Das Reich divisions had wheeled eastward toward Prokhorovka, destroying units of the Fifth Guards Army as they advanced and sending the First Tank and Sixth Guards armies tumbling back before them.

Eight days of nonstop fighting had left Hoth's grimy panzer crewmen near exhaustion and short of ammunition, and their machines in need of repair. Still, the battle appeared to be developing well. In anticipation of the final push on Kursk, Manstein began moving his reserve, the XXIV Panzer Corps, consisting of the 23d Panzer Division and the SS Wiking Division, into an assembly area outside Belgorod.

But the Germans had not taken into account the vast numbers of Red Army reserves. A few days earlier, Stalin had ordered the Steppe Front's Fifth Guards Tank Army of General Pavel Rotmistrov to proceed by forced march to an assembly area located northeast of Prokhorovka. By the night of July 11, Rotmistrov's forces had completed the 225-mile journey and were ready to lead a counterattack against Hoth's SS forces.

As the Germans advanced the following morning, July 12, they were expecting to encounter only a few slow-moving brigades of KV heavy tanks, other armor in fixed positions, and some antitank guns in the hills outside Prokhorovka. Instead, Hoth's battle-weary force of some 600 tanks, including 100 Tigers, collided head-on with Rotmistrov's fresh tank army, 850 tanks strong, almost all of them T-34s.

A panzer officer recalled the moment: "We found ourselves taking on a seemingly inexhaustible mass of enemy armor. The clouds of dust made it difficult to get help from the Luftwaffe, and soon many of the T-34s had broken past our screen and were streaming like rats all over the battlefield."

For eight hours, the battle raged back and forth in stifling heat. The closeness of the fighting favored the T-34s. Using their greater maneuverability, the Soviet tanks rumbled in and out of the German columns,

General Walther Model, commander of the Ninth Army of Army Group Center, issues instructions to two members of his staff near Orel, eighty miles north of Kursk. Model's forces struggled through the first line of Soviet defenses on the opening day of battle, but then ground to a halt on July 12 after advancing only twelve miles.

isolating the heavier Tigers from the Panthers and Panzer IVs and destroying them at close range. The battlefield became an inferno of wrecked and flaming armor. Directly overhead, German and Soviet ground-support planes desperately tried to distinguish friend from foe, while high above them, the fighters of both sides fought their own screaming battles. The day ended in a stalemate, with both sides losing more than 300 tanks.

Hoth himself had arrived at the front during the afternoon. From a forward position with the Das Reich Division, he placed an urgent call back to his chief of staff at Fourth Panzer Army headquarters: "Have you any news of Kempf? Where is his III Panzer Corps?"

The answer came back instantly. Kempf was only twelve miles away at

Rzhavets, on the east side of the Donets. He would be arriving in full force the next day, with nearly 300 tanks and assault guns, perhaps enough to tip the scales in Hoth's favor.

But Kempf would never get the opportunity to do so. While the titanic tank battle had been raging at Prokhorovka, a disaster had befallen Army Group Center in the northern sector. With Model's forces pinned down outside Olkhovatka, the Soviet West and the Bryansk fronts had come roaring out of the northern edge of the Orel salient against the weakened Second Panzer Army that was defending Model's rear. The Ninth Army suddenly had to shift to the defensive. The German pincers movement had been shorn of its northern jaw.

When Army Detachment Kempf arrived at the smoking battlefield of Prokhorovka on July 13, it was all for naught. That very day, Hitler summoned Manstein and Kluge to Wolfsschanze in East Prussia to tell them further bad news. The Allies had landed on Sicily three days earlier, and the Führer could concentrate on nothing else. With Citadel's outcome still uncertain, he had made up his mind to abandon the offensive in order to rush reinforcements to Italy and the western Balkans.

Manstein was furious. He insisted that the battle had just reached its turning point and that the invasion of Sicily was a small matter in comparison with the immediate crisis at Kursk. Even though Army Group Center could play no further offensive role, Army Group South had the upper hand in its mortal struggle with the Soviets' mobile reserves. By smashing them, he could forestall future counteroffensives in other sectors of the front and buy valuable time. Manstein urged Hitler to order the Ninth Army to tie down sufficient Soviet divisions on the northern front so that he could finish the job in the south. One of Manstein's generals aptly summed up the situation: "We are in the position of a man who had seized a wolf by the ears and dared not let him go."

Kluge was uncooperative, however. He insisted that the Ninth Army had to withdraw to its starting line. All that Manstein got from Hitler was permission to continue the offensive independently. But a few days later, Hitler changed his mind. He ordered Manstein to shift Grossdeutschland to Army Group Center and take II SS Panzer Corps out of the line. He wanted to transfer the politically indoctrinated SS men to Italy to backstop the shaky Italian Army.

Thus weakened, Manstein foresaw that it was impossible to hold his gains in the Kursk salient, and he ordered his forces to return to the vicinity of Belgorod. The misfired offensive had cost the Germans between 20,000 and 30,000 dead and wounded, as well as hundreds of guns, aircraft, and trucks. None of them could be easily replaced. Although the Soviet battle

With shells bursting around them and corpses and abandoned weapons littering the ground, German soldiers hug the wall of an antitank ditch during the fighting for Kursk.

On July 12, smoke billows from burning tanks and downed planes as Panzer IV tanks from Hausser's II SS Panzer Corps roll forward to battle the Fifth Guards Tank Army near Prokhorovka, approximately thirty miles north of Belgorod.

losses were never disclosed, they were probably comparable, if not higher.

The long delay before the battle had failed to provide sufficient time in which to work out the kinks in Hitler's superweapons, and the unforgiving environment of the battlefield had proved a poor testing ground. The Ferdinand self-propelled assault gun was a total flop. Its tracks were weak and its powerful 88-mm gun unsuited for close-range fighting. Those guns that were not halted by mechanical failures were destroyed by Soviet infantrymen. Of the hapless Ferdinands, Guderian reported, "Once they had broken into the enemy's infantry zone they literally had to go quail shooting with cannon. They did not manage to neutralize, let alone destroy, the enemy rifles and machine guns, so that the infantry was unable to follow up behind them. By the time they reached the Russian artillery, they were on their own."

The Panther tanks also were a great disappointment. Their narrow tracks caused them to become bogged down in swampy bottom land, and their inexperienced crews had a hard time keeping them in formation. Another ballyhooed weapon, the Hornet antitank assault gun, could not even be used because the support brackets were inadequate.

Stalin was quick to exploit Hitler's failed gamble. On July 17, the South-West and South fronts crashed across the Mius River toward Stalino and Taganrog along the northern coast of the Sea of Azov in an attempt to cut off Field Marshal Ewald von Kleist's Army Group A on Manstein's southern flank. When Manstein shifted his reserves south to assist Kleist, he left himself too weak to deal with General Vatutin's Voronezh Front. At the same time, Kluge was being pushed back toward Smolensk, leaving Army Group Center unable to help Manstein. For the German army, the war had

"A Concert of Hell"

At Kursk, Soviet antitank and assault guns appear in the periscope *(below)* of a commander in the Waffen-SS Panzer Division Das Reich. Tank crews painted distinctive emblems on their vehicles; those of Das Reich were identified by an arrangement of runic symbols *(right).*

From inside a tank, the battle for Kursk was a "concert of hell," according to a gunner who served aboard a Tiger in one of Hitler's panzer divisions. The five crewmen of a panzer—commander, radio operator, driver, gunner, and loader—were pounded by Soviet fire, deafened by the growl of their vehicle's engine, and blind to the battle outside except for what was visible through periscopes and small ports. Yet the men hunched inside one of these metal monsters managed to perform an intricate drill.

On spotting a target through his periscope or one of five horizontal viewing slits, the tank commander, seated in the turret, barked directions through an intercom to the driver in the hull below. The radio operator, seated opposite the driver, turned from his set and took charge of a machine gun. On the commander's order, the loader, seated in the turret, grabbed a round from the nearest ammo bin, rammed it into the tank's 88-mm gun, and closed the breech. The driver halted when he was within range of the target. The gunner carefully aimed his weapon using controls in the turret and, when his superior gave the word, fired.

So familiar was this drill that the men could act almost before an order was given. At Kursk, however, such expertise did not bring them victory. The panzer crews were plagued by conditions beyond their control: swampy soil that bogged down their vehicles, acre after acre of Soviet minefields that blew away the tank treads, and swarms of nimble T-34 tanks that added their firepower to the Soviet defense. The Tigers had met their match, and Hitler's offensive was stopped.

A Tiger commander surveys a battlefield through the turret hatch. Because of noise from the battle and the engine of his own tank, he communicated with his crew via intercom.

His vision limited to what could be seen through either a periscope or the slot above the steering wheel, the driver *(below)* maneuvered with the assistance of his commander.

A loader *(right)* holds an 88-mm shell. One tanker wrote that after laying a round into the breech, he would give it a "stroke and a wish on its way."

A radio operator *(below)* adjusts his set. As a vital communications link, he received and sent messages to the unit commander as well as to other tanks.

Using the telescopic sight beside him and following instructions from the commander, the gunner aimed and fired the tank's cannon.

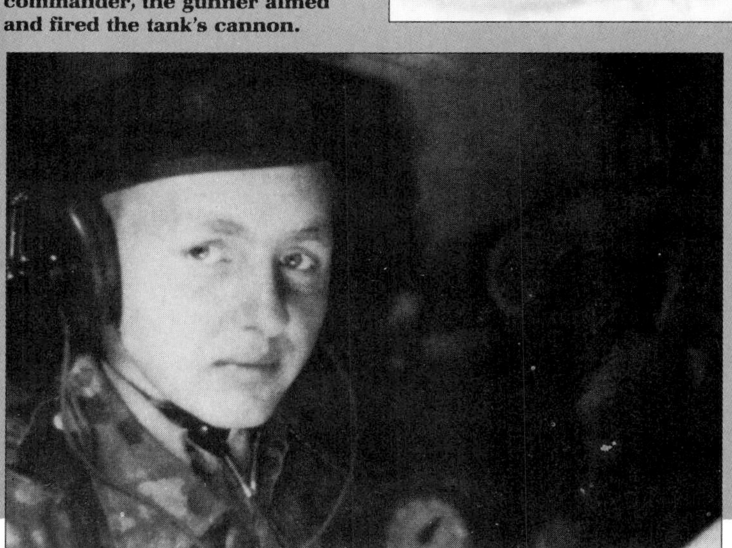

North of Kursk, in the German salient centered on Orel, Russian soldiers oblivious to the bodies around them charge through a German position that has been decimated by artillery during the Russian counterattack.

become a desperate defensive struggle consisting of stopgap measures against a much stronger enemy.

On August 3, Vatutin unleashed a two-pronged offensive with five full armies against Manstein's forces north of Belgorod. This force was proof of the extraordinary depth of Soviet reserves, scarcely three weeks after the horrendous Russian losses in the fight for Kursk. The Red Army now claimed fourfold superiority in guns and tanks. Behind the attacking rifle divisions, two tank armies got in between Hoth's Fourth Panzer Army and Army Detachment Kempf and penetrated deep into the German defenses.

The reserves that Manstein was able to bring forward were not enough, and Belgorod had to be abandoned.

The news was no better in the north, where the Russians threatened to encircle the Second Panzer Army, now under Model's command. Preoccupied with the crisis in Italy, Hitler had given Model permission to conduct an "elastic defense," which included the freedom to surrender the Orel salient and withdraw behind the Desna River, if necessary. Model promptly ordered both the Second Panzer Army and the Ninth Army back to a series of defensive works, called the Hagen Line, that had been prepared across the neck of the Orel salient. The Hagen Line guarded the vital junction of Bryansk, where the north-south and east-west railroads joined behind Army Group Center.

Stalin sensed that the tide had turned decisively, and he ordered a celebratory artillery salvo in Moscow the night of August 5. Belgorod and

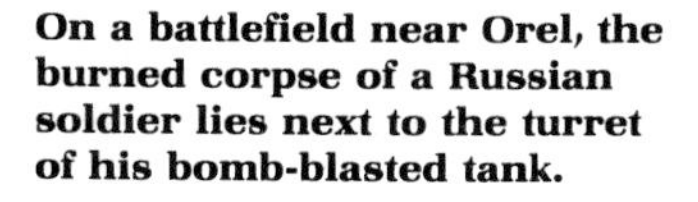

On a battlefield near Orel, the burned corpse of a Russian soldier lies next to the turret of his bomb-blasted tank.

A Soviet soldier marches his German captive through a village near Orel. On August 5, Josef Stalin announced that the Red Army had complete control of Orel and Belgorod. "I express my thanks to all the troops that took part in the offensive," he proclaimed. "Eternal glory to the heroes who fell in the struggle for the freedom of our country."

Orel were back in Soviet hands, and the prospects were enhanced for achieving the larger objective of pushing Army Group South back from the Dnieper River to the Sea of Azov where it could be destroyed. With that accomplished, one of Hitler's most cherished conquests, the resource-rich Ukraine, would be lost to the Germans.

By the second week of August, the Russians were pouring through a thirty-four-mile-wide gap in the German line southwest of the Kursk salient between Hoth's Fourth Panzers and Army Detachment Kempf, threatening to reclaim Kharkov yet again. The German effort to retain the much-fought-over city was a forlorn one, given the pressing need to withdraw and form a defensive line to the west.

Hitler feared the political repercussions among his Axis partners if Kharkov fell, however. His orders to hold the city "at all costs" left Manstein no choice. On the Führer's command, Manstein moved General Erhard Raus's provisional corps into the city. The Austrian Raus was a highly experienced tank commander, but after weeks of continuous combat, his men were at the breaking point. Manstein ordered the 3d Panzer Division to move up on Raus's exposed left flank to reinforce Raus's four divisions and the elements of the Fourth Panzer Army under his command. But to the northwest, Vatutin's forces were moving through the gap unimpeded, driving to link up with Konev's forces of the Steppe Front. Together, the two Soviet army groups would encircle Kharkov.

If there was anything left in the Ukrainian city worth fighting for, besides Hitler's pride, it was the immense store of supplies the Germans had accumulated there for Army Group South. There were enough provisions for three months, everything from ammunition and spare parts to boxes of cigars and cases of fine French cognac.

Almost miraculously in the middle of a major withdrawal, transport materialized to move the bulk of these supplies to Army Detachment Kempf, now called the Eighth Army. Just about everything was evacuated from the supply centers in and around Kharkov—everything except the great carboys of Russian vodka. The alcohol was temptation too much for the arriving Soviet soldiers. It slowed them down for forty-eight hours, a godsend to the beleaguered Manstein. The respite was time enough for him to bring up the SS Wiking Division to protect Raus's northern flank and save Kharkov for a few more days.

Finally, Manstein made the inevitable decision. "I am not prepared to sacrifice six divisions for some questionable political consideration," he said, and in disobedience to Hitler, he ordered Raus to withdraw. But before the city returned for the final time to Russian hands on August 23, Raus made them pay dearly for it in blood.

Hitler reluctantly accepted Manstein's decision to withdraw because he wanted to leave tactical control on the eastern front in the capable hands of the field marshal. For his part, Manstein recognized that Stalin's objective was clearly larger than the ruins of the once-great city. Nearly all of Army Group South and Kleist's Army Group A were now under heavy attack. To survive, both forces would have to retreat to the next defensible line—the Dnieper River.

Over the next few weeks, Manstein managed to check the Russians by a series of small, well-aimed counterattacks, gaining breathing space in order to prepare the retreat. But by then, it was too late to stem the Soviet flood. The failure of Operation Citadel and the subsequent fall of Kharkov signaled the beginning of a long German withdrawal westward that would not end until it reached Berlin.

TWO

Ebb Tide in the East

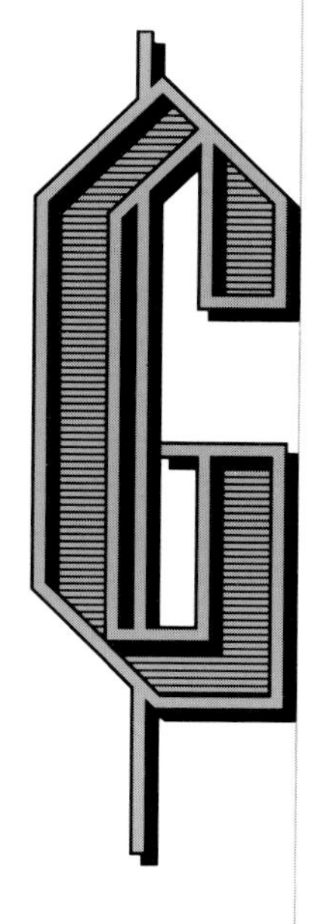

erman commanders on the eastern front in the hot, dusty late summer of 1943 faced two vexing obstacles to success: One, of course, was the enemy, the growing hordes of Soviet troops with their ever-increasing store of armaments. The other problem lay behind the German lines, and could be said to be an internal one. The problem was Adolf Hitler.

Despite dwindling numbers of German troops, Wehrmacht generals remained confident they could grind the enemy down and at least fight to a stalemate—if only the Führer would allow them to conduct operations unfettered. But the moves that could stymie the Russians were exactly what Hitler was by nature unable to permit—retreats, carried out to shorten or straighten lines, eliminate vulnerable salients, prevent encirclements.

"Hitler always tried to make us fight for every yard, threatening to court-martial anyone who didn't," said General Siegfried Henrici, XL Panzer Corps commander. "No withdrawal was officially permitted without his approval—even a small-scale withdrawal. Time after time, forces stayed in impossible positions until they were surrounded and captured." So tightly did Hitler control troop movements, Henrici asserted, that "battalion commanders were afraid to move a sentry from the window to the door."

The losses caused by Hitler's stubbornness were bleeding the German army, pitting it against the Soviets in a war of numbers it could not win. By the end of August, many of the German commands along the now-1,200-mile eastern front between the Gulf of Finland and the Sea of Azov faced overwhelming odds. On the north, Field Marshal Georg von Küchler's Army Group North was still laying siege to Leningrad, and there was little movement. But opposite Field Marshal Günther Hans von Kluge's Army Group Center and Field Marshal Erich von Manstein's Army Group South, eight massive Soviet fronts were primed for action, fielding a combined strength of 3.8 million men, 4,000 tanks, 70,000 guns, and 3,750 aircraft. To hold them off, the Germans, after the bloodletting of Operation Citadel and the Soviet summer offensive, could muster only about 1.24 million front-line combat troops, 2,400 tanks and self-propelled guns, 12,600 artillery pieces, and 2,000 planes.

Rising starkly above the smoldering remains of the city of Kremenchug, an ornate Orthodox church captures the attention of a group of German soldiers. The building was unaccountably exempted from the scorched earth order imposed by Hitler on Army Group South as it withdrew from the Ukraine in August of 1943.

Since the previous November, the number of German units in the East had changed little, but many individual units were below strength—some drastically so. New levies from home, furthermore, were not up to the quality of the troops that had slashed through the Red Army to the doorstep of Leningrad, Moscow, and Stalingrad. A new term was gaining currency—*Krisenfestigkeit,* meaning the "ability to withstand crises." The toughest German divisions were rated *krisenfest,* "steadfast in critical situations." Fewer and fewer of them now warranted that honorific.

Veteran forces continued to perform well, maintaining the German capacity to overcome numerical superiority with mobility and generalship. But in the late summer of 1943, skillful leadership was no longer enough. German forces facing the Russians were stretched to the breaking point, and Field Marshal von Manstein's Army Group South, in particular, would soon be dealt a massive blow.

After his withdrawal from Kharkov in August, Manstein had managed to hold off a Soviet breakthrough to Poltava, to the southwest. But he remained in jeopardy. His Fourth Panzer Army faced the Soviet Voronezh Front, which consisted of three armies poised for the assault and a fourth in reserve, all under General Nikolay Vatutin, an opponent whose strategic skills approached Manstein's own. Equally daunting was the fact that Manstein's Eighth Army was lined up against General Ivan Konev's Steppe Front with its six armies.

Ordered by OKH—the army high command—to stand firm in defense of the Donets Basin, Manstein wrote to Hitler at Wolfsschanze in East Prussia, stating in his characteristically blunt way that only with massive reinforcements could he defend the region. "I request freedom of maneuver," Manstein added. But Hitler invariably understood "freedom of maneuver" to mean freedom to relinquish territory, a thought he could not accept. His reply came by telephone: "Don't do anything. I am coming myself."

They met on August 27 at Vinnitsa in the Ukraine, which had been Hitler's forward headquarters in palmier days. The woods around Vinnitsa were close and hot that summer, and Hitler was unhappy, disagreeable, and suspicious there. His ill feelings were probably heightened by the awareness that the once-secure location only about seventy-five miles west of the Dnieper River now lay in the path of a gathering Soviet offensive.

Manstein pointed out to Hitler that his Army Group South had lost 133,000 soldiers in the past few months and had received only 33,000 replacements. Then he asked General Karl Hollidt, who had been in command at many crucial points along the eastern front, to give the Führer a comparative picture of each side's strength. Hollidt described the reduced circumstances of his Sixth Army, which was lined up against Soviet General

Field Marshal Erich von Manstein, commander of Army Group South, meets with Hitler on September 8, 1943, at Manstein's headquarters in Zaporozhe. In a series of meetings over several weeks, Manstein argued strategy with an obdurate Hitler, finally winning grudging permission for a withdrawal behind the Dnieper River.

Fyodor Tolbukhin's South Front: The XXIX Corps had 8,706 men facing an estimated 69,000 Soviets; the XVII Corps, 9,284 men facing 49,500; the IV Corps—"relatively best off"—13,143 men facing 18,000. In armament, 7 tanks and 38 assault guns of the Sixth Army confronted 165 Soviet tanks.

Manstein then summed it up for Hitler. "With our available forces, the Donets region cannot be defended, my Führer. Either you let us have fresh forces, and that means twelve divisions, or the Donets region must be abandoned. I see no other solution." Hitler hesitated, evaded, and argued that every inch of ground must be contested to avoid the intolerable loss of the region's industrial and agricultural riches. Finally, to Manstein's satisfaction, Hitler promised reinforcements.

But Manstein's sense of relief was short lived. The day before the Vinnitsa meeting began, Soviet General Konstantin Rokossovsky had launched his Central Front on an offensive against Kluge's Army Group Center, which was the anticipated source of the reinforcements Manstein had demanded. On August 28, Kluge in his turn went personally to Hitler to protest any proposed transfer of his own harried forces to Manstein's command. In the end, despite Hitler's promises, Manstein received nothing.

In the southern sector of Army Group South, Hollidt's Sixth Army, ground down by combat losses and the removal of some of its best divisions, was thinly stretched over a front of 120 miles running along the Mius River to the Sea of Azov at Taganrog. In late August, two fast-moving corps of the Soviet South Front crashed through Hollidt's lines and wheeled southward toward Mariupol, on the Sea of Azov. When a narrow gap opened in the German front near Kuibyshevo, General Tolbukhin unhesitatingly poured division after division through it and sent them racing to the coast at Taganrog, trapping the German XXIX Corps against the sea. The corps's divisions managed to break out of the encirclement only through desperate fighting at several spots. At that point, Manstein demanded and at last received Hitler's grudging consent—"provided there is no other possible alternative," was the way the Führer put it—to pull the Sixth Army back some forty miles, to the Tortoise Line, an inadequate defensive work built earlier by German engineers to protect the industrial city of Stalino.

The price for Hitler's alternating obstinacy and vacillation was already being paid in forced German retreats all along the line. At the end of August, Rokossovsky's three Central Front armies, attacking from what had been the western boundary of the Kursk salient, charged toward the Desna River, opening a fifty-mile-wide gap between Army Group Center and Army Group South within a week. Together with Vatutin's Voronezh Front, Rokossovsky's forces drove toward Kiev, the capital of the Ukraine and a main transportation hub on the Dnieper. The South-West Front of General Rodion Malinovsky also pushed westward, ripping open the just-occupied Tortoise Line between General Eberhard von Mackensen's First Panzer Army and Hollidt's Sixth Army, while Malinovsky's armor raced toward the Dnieper bridgeheads at Dnepropetrovsk. The Soviet units moving to encircle Manstein never stopped to rest, regroup, or consolidate, taking their cue from Stalin himself, who cheered them on with the cry, "Smash Army Group South—that's the key to victory."

On September 8, Hitler flew to Manstein's headquarters at Zaporozhe, on the Dnieper, burdened with bad news from the southern flank of Europe: Italy had surrendered to the Allies that day. But Manstein had different concerns. This time he was accompanied by Field Marshal Ewald von Kleist, commander of Army Group A in the Crimean peninsula, and General Erwin Jaenecke, commander of the Seventeenth Army, which clung to Hitler's last remaining foothold in the Caucusus—the Taman Peninsula, across the Kerch Strait from the Crimea. Manstein told Hitler that barring a withdrawal, the envelopment of Army Group South was a certainty. Army Group A and the Seventeenth Army would be cut off far to the south, and Manstein would be unable to help them. "Then two armies will be lost, my Führer," Manstein said, "and nothing can ever bring them back again."

Although Stalino fell to the Soviets that day, and Mariupol two days later, Hitler again rejected Manstein's request for permission to withdraw from the Donets. Instead, he again promised reinforcements—this time two

Soviet officers watch as their troops advance against the artillery fire of the German Seventeenth Army in the Kuban peninsula, between the Sea of Azov and the Black Sea. When the Soviet forces pushed the Germans out of the Kuban in September 1943, the peninsula became the jumping-off place for a drive to liberate the Crimea.

panzer and two infantry divisions from Army Group Center and four divisions from the Seventeenth Army. Again, the promises were not kept. Manstein dispatched an angry message to Hitler through the chief of the OKH general staff, General Kurt Zeitzler: "Kindly inform the Führer that he may expect the beginning of a disastrous Soviet breakthrough to the Dnieper at any moment."

One week later, the accuracy of Manstein's forecast became apparent. The Soviet breakthrough was already taking shape. The thrusts spreading out like fingers from the center of the Soviet line around Kharkov were growing ever longer. Divisions of Vatutin's Voronezh Front had broken through between the XXIV Panzer Corps and the Eighth Army on Manstein's northern wing and were positioned seventy-five miles from the Dnieper at Cherkassy. Rokossovsky's Central Front, which was pressuring the Fourth Panzer Army of General Hermann Hoth, had driven within forty-six miles of Kiev. And Tolbukhin's South Front was closing in on the Sea of Azov, threatening to trap the Sixth Army around Nikopol and the Seventeenth Army in the Crimea.

If there had ever been a chance to halt the Soviets east of the Dnieper by bringing up reserves, it was lost by the time Manstein and Hitler met yet again, on September 15, at Wolfsschanze. "What is at stake now, my Führer, is the fate of the eastern front," Manstein said. At that too-late hour, Hitler finally acquiesced to Manstein's demand for freedom to maneuver as he saw fit. That same day, Manstein ordered his forces to start their great withdrawal to the west bank of the Dnieper from north of Kiev to Zaporozhe, and to the Wotan Line the rest of the way south to the Sea of Azov.

In every way, the Dnieper was a critical target. The great river, at about 1,400 miles the third-longest in Europe, rises northeast of Smolensk and slices through the eastern half of Belorussia as it flows southward to Kiev. From there, it runs through the Ukraine, heading southeast, then south from near Dnepropetrovsk to Zaporozhe, and finally southwest to the Black Sea. On the banks of the Dnieper, Russia was born; its waters make the Ukraine the country's granary. Iron, manganese, copper, and nickel deposits lie within its great bend around Krivoi Rog, Zaporozhe, and Nikopol. More than 30 percent of Germany's raw materials for manufacturing munitions came from those sources.

Militarily, the Dnieper offered the Germans the possibility of averting disaster. The general staff depended on its great cliffs, rising several hundred feet high at some points on the west bank, and its wide stretches, at places more than half a mile across, to help them stop the Russians.

To overcome that barrier, Stalin mobilized one of the most powerful concentrations of force amassed during the war. Forty percent of the Red Army's infantry and 84 percent of its armored forces were to be thrown against Army Group South. The outcome of the struggle that had begun June 22, 1941, with the launching of Operation Barbarossa, Hitler's invasion of the Soviet Union, was to be determined along the Dnieper's waters.

From his headquarters at Zaporozhe, Manstein laid out the general plan for holding off the Soviets. His principle guiding the pullback to the river was that "as long as units remain intact, they will overcome every difficulty, whereas no withdrawal can be carried out with troops who have lost their fighting strength or stability."

Still, the Germans had begun what was to become a vast, complex, and bitter exodus. Manstein was maneuvering battle-weary troops under pressure from superior ground forces and under air attack from an improving Soviet air force. His four armies totaled one million men—organized into fifteen corps comprising sixty-three divisions, equipped with tanks, trucks, and horses. He was also responsible for some 200,000 wounded.

Manstein had orders to leave nothing behind but scorched earth as he withdrew. The Germans intended to collect all available booty for the Reich

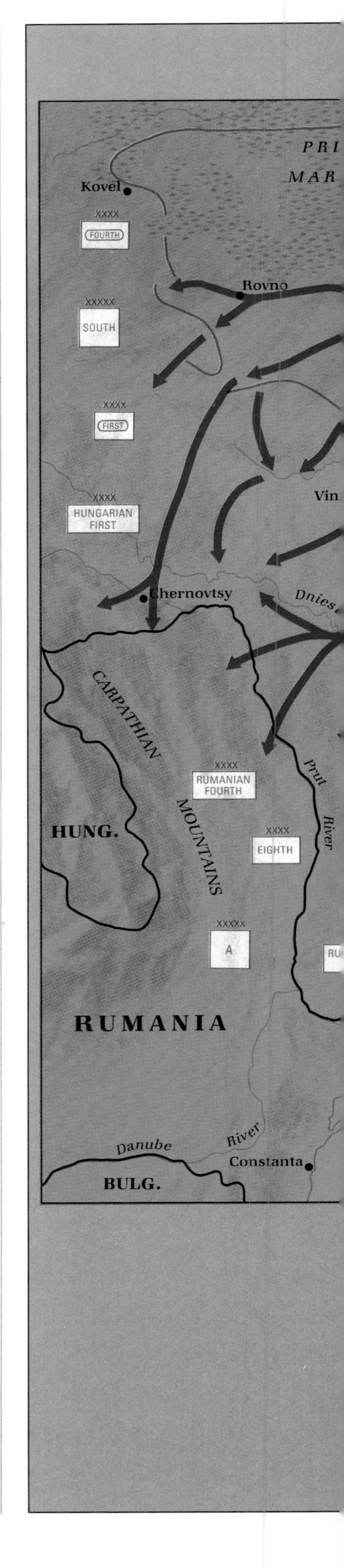

The Race for the Dnieper

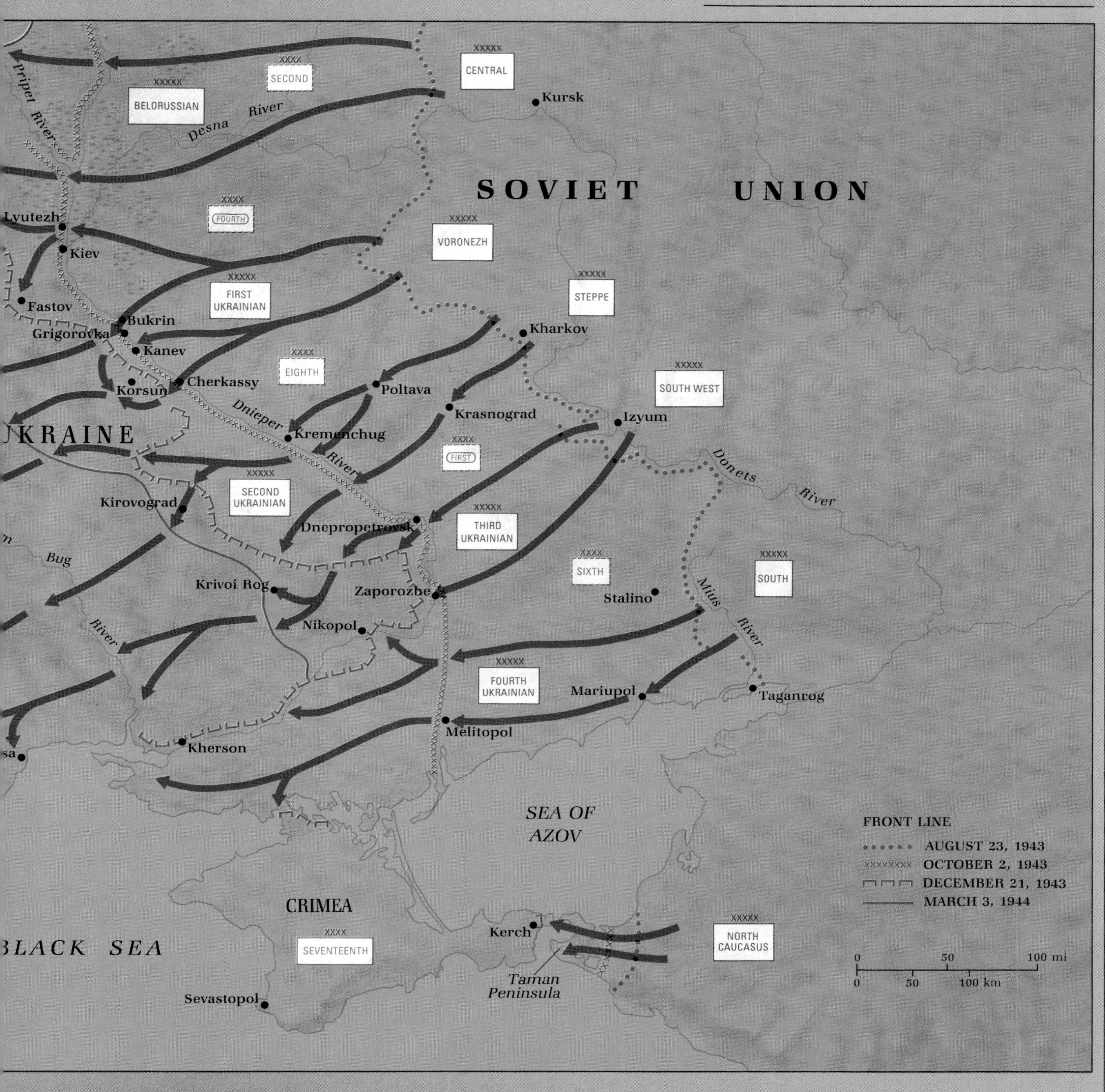

Following the failure of the German bid to capture Kursk and the subsequent Russian counterattack in August 1943, Field Marshal Erich von Manstein ordered Army Group South to withdraw to the Dnieper River and establish a defensive line on its east bank. By the end of September, however, hopes of defending the Dnieper vanished when the Soviet Voronezh, Steppe, and South-West fronts crossed the river at more than twenty-six points. By year's end, the entire Dnieper was in Russian hands, and the German Seventeenth Army was cut off on the Crimean peninsula. A nonstop Soviet winter offensive in 1943 continued to push the beleaguered Germans westward through the Ukraine. In February 1944, more than 60,000 Germans were trapped in the Cherkassy pocket. By the time Hitler dismissed Manstein on March 31, the Red Army had forced the Germans into Bessarabia and Galicia, more than 300 miles west of their starting position eight months earlier.

and then destroy anything that could be of use to the advancing Red Army. A message from Reich Marshal Hermann Göring, acting on Hitler's authority in his role as commissioner for the German Four-Year Plan, instructed Manstein that a zone fifteen miles deep along the east bank of the Dnieper was "to be emptied of all provisions, economic goods, and machinery." As he fell back, Manstein wrote later, he therefore took "every possible measure likely to impede the enemy. It was now necessary for the Germans, too, to resort to the 'scorched earth' policy that the Soviets had adopted during their retreats of previous years."

Since the Germans knew that the Soviet armies were conscripting local men between the ages of sixteen and sixty to be instant front-line soldiers, Manstein rounded them up first. About 200,000 men of military age, as well as industrial and agricultural workers, were swept up by the German armies and herded west. Some went willingly, so dreading the return of Stalin's rule that they chose to abandon their own country and throw in their lot with the enemy.

Some 2,500 trains were required to shift expropriated Soviet property, as well as German equipment and supplies, to the Dnieper. The rail cars carried grain and other farm products, tractors, threshing machines, machine tools, and damaged tanks. Vast numbers of animals—200,000 cattle, 270,000 sheep, and 153,000 horses in addition to the army's own—became part of Manstein's booty. With the herds of animals, about 40,000 loaded peasant carts went bumping along the roads to the Dnieper. The migration raised vast clouds of dust. Describing the immensity of the scene to his family at home, a lieutenant from Hamburg called it "exciting and unreal, curious and grim. A country and an army," he wrote, "are on the move."

As his armies headed for the Dnieper, often under heavy attack from the Soviets, Manstein on September 18 issued orders for their defensive alignment along its west bank. The two southern corps of the Sixth Army were not actually to cross the river but were to dig in behind prepared defensive positions on the Wotan Line, which began at Zaporozhe, where the Dnieper turns away to the southwest, and extended due south to Melitopol. The Sixth Army's northern corps was to aim for Zaporozhe. The First Panzer Army was to withdraw to the river between Zaporozhe and Dnepropetrovsk. The Eighth Army was ordered to pull back to the sector around Kremenchug and Cherkassy. The Fourth Panzer Army's assignment was the stretch running from Kanev for seventy-five miles upriver to Kiev, and north of Kiev to the Pripet River, the boundary between Army Groups South and Center.

Once they reached the Dnieper, all these formations would have to narrow down from the width of a 450-mile front to converge on just five sectors where bridges stood or could be laid down relatively quickly—at Kiev, Kanev, Cherkassy, Kremenchug, and Dnepropetrovsk. And once across, they would have to fan out again. Only when they were fully deployed for 450 miles along the west bank could they hope to defend the river's reaches against the advancing Russians.

Heroics, horror, and death marked the movement of German forces to the west over the next few days. As so often in the past, Manstein's Fourth Panzer Army was at the center of the fighting, taking losses and inflicting them with unflinching courage. Its VII and XIII corps, hard pressed by the Russians, were battling to reach the German bridgehead at Kiev. The Fourth Panzer's XXIV Corps, separated from the main body of the army, was heading toward Kanev under the command of General Walther Nehring.

A German military column of trucks and horse-drawn wagons moves slowly down a dusty road toward the Dnieper during the retreat of Army Group South in the late summer of 1943. By this time, the once-vaunted German war machine was relying more heavily on horse-drawn transport than was the Red Army.

The Luftwaffe's Ace Tank Killer

The undisputed Luftwaffe ace of the eastern front, Hans-Ulrich Rudel specialized in killing Soviet T-34 tanks. His string of spectacular successes as a pilot of the Ju 87 Stuka dive bomber began early in the war when he sank a Soviet battleship with a single bomb. Soon afterward, he began experimenting with a Stuka specially armed as a tank destroyer. Perfecting the technique of attacking low and from the rear, he knocked out 519 Russian tanks, sometimes flying as many as seventeen sorties a day in support of the German armies on the collapsing eastern front. A die-hard admirer of Hitler and a relentless foe of bolshevism, Rudel flew his final few missions without a right leg, which had been amputated after nearly being severed by Soviet flak three months before the end of the war.

Che pendant of Hans-Ulrich Rudel's Flying Clasp shows that ıe flew more than 2,000 nissions—the most by far of any Luftwaffe pilot. The clasp was made of gold, the wreath and swords were of platinum, and the mission count was executed in tiny diamonds.

n the cockpit of his Ju 87G *(left)*, Rudel salutes before taking off on a mission in 1943. His ank-killer version of the Stuka was divested of its siren, dive brakes, and bomb racks, and armed instead with two 37-mm lak cannon loaded with special armor-piercing ammunition.

Rudel shows fellow pilots the best way to attack Soviet T-34 anks *(far left)*. Because the T-34's hinnest armor was at the rear, around the engine compartment, German pilots developed a echnique of blasting the rearmost tank in a battle formation and then sweeping back around to attack the next one.

Of the 15 million Germans who ook up arms in World War II, only Rudel won the Third Reich's highest military medal, he Knight's Cross with Golden Oak Leaves, Swords, and Diamonds *(left)*, presented to him by Hitler on January 1, 1945.

But racing the XXIV Corps to the Kanev-Kiev region was the spearhead of the approaching Soviet forces, General Rybalko's Third Guards Tank Army. Rybalko was using a favorite Russian tactic—attacking at the gaps between German units to gain ground cheaply by avoiding head-on clashes. The method was particularly effective during the retreat of Army Group South, because huge gaps opened between contracting German divisions as they approached the river crossings.

During the rush to the river, General Otto Wöhler's Eighth Army intercepted an uncoded message from a partisan group informing other partisans that no retreating German forces had yet shown up on the west bank of the Dnieper between Kanev and Kiev. Wöhler immediately guessed that General Vatutin possessed this accurate information and was planning a daring strike somewhere along that stretch of river, hoping to establish his forces there before units of the Fourth Panzer or the Eighth Army could arrive to take up defensive positions.

To forestall that effort, Wöhler ordered a quick thrust to the area by the closest German force, which turned out to be a small weapons training center at Cherkassy, just to the southeast of Kanev. Awakened in the middle of the night, the 120 men from the center were rumbling along toward Kanev in trucks within a couple of hours.

But the Soviets, acting on the partisan tip, had already arrived at the river. Four volunteers, privates in a Third Guards Tank Army company commanded by a lieutenant named Sinashkin, were hidden among half-submerged reeds along the riverbank, signaling each other by imitating the call of the bittern. They joined up with a partisan who was familiar with the territory and slipped aboard a concealed skiff to cross over and launch a diversionary attack. Using muffled oars, they landed several hundred yards north of the village of Grigorovka. Once there, they opened fire on German pickets. Moving rapidly from one spot to another, crashing around, they made enough commotion for a battalion.

The ruse provided cover for a larger crossing half a mile to the north. There, the bulk of Lieutenant Sinashkin's company had nailed together planks and barrels as makeshift rafts. While the German sentries were occupied with the few noisy soldiers downstream, Sinashkin and his men floated across the Dnieper. By the morning of September 22 they, along with 120 partisans, had established their bridgehead. From Kanev north almost to Kiev, sixty miles of river front on the west bank now lay wide open to the Soviets if they could bring sufficient forces to bear; there was no German combat unit worth the name in that whole stretch of territory. Nehring's XXIV Panzer Corps, assigned to spread out and defend this sector after crossing at Kanev, was still struggling toward the east bank.

Forces available to General Wöhler for an immediate counterattack consisted only of the 120 men from the weapons training center. But reinforcements soon came from the 19th Panzer Division, part of which had crossed the Dnieper at Kiev. An armored reconnaissance battalion from the 19th, commanded by Major Kurt Guderian, younger son of the renowned panzer general, raced to Grigorovka to enter the fray. Wöhler ordered General Nehring to rush his troops across the main bridge at Kanev to help wipe out the Soviet enclave. General Rybalko answered by launching forty-four T-34 tanks against Nehring's bridgehead on the east bank, intending to seize the span and block the XXIV Corps from crossing. Only heroic efforts by handfuls of German troops with antitank weapons managed finally to stop the tank attack.

That threat disposed of, Nehring poured reinforcements for the 19th Panzer Division across the bridge. His engineers had built a second deck atop the original railroad span so that train traffic could continue while vehicles and men crossed overhead. After his divisions sped across the Dnieper—Nehring himself was the last man over—engineers demolished the bridge with explosives. The Germans had won this particular race, and the troublesome Soviet bridgehead north of Kanev was soon contained.

Elsewhere along the river, other Soviet probes threatened Manstein's plan to defend the west bank. About the same time as Sinashkin's landing, the Soviet Thirteenth Army was nearing the river 120 miles to the north, in the swampy area where the Pripet River joins the Dnieper at Chernigov. This boggy terrain, precisely in the zone between Army Group South and Army Group Center, seemed an unlikely choice for a landing—except that, once again, partisan activity had paved the way. The partisans had laid concealed roads through the Pripet Marshes, and along them came Russian troops, forming a bridgehead across the Dnieper on September 26.

By the end of September, the Soviets had crossed the river in twenty-three places from Loyev, 100 miles north of Kiev, to Zaporozhe, 450 miles to the south. Most of the crossings resembled the small, improvised affair at Grigorovka. At Stayki, near Bukrin, for instance, a fifty-man force had crossed only to find itself under heavy attack by the 34th Infantry Division. It could make no headway, yet it proved very difficult to dislodge from its firing pits and high parapets. These small bridgeheads were of little use to the Soviets unless they could be expanded into bases that would provide a means of ferrying troops, tanks, trucks, and artillery across the river.

While digging in against one of these Soviet enclaves near Grigorovka at dusk on the 24th, a battalion of the German 258th Infantry Regiment heard the cry, "Enemy aircraft." The men dived for cover, but the huge formation of planes passing overhead neither bombed nor strafed. The planes were

A German aerial reconnaissance photograph of the Red Army's Bukrin bridgehead across the Dnieper, taken October 20, 1943, shows that two bridges—marked *7a* and *7b*—have been knocked out. Four days after the photograph was taken, the Soviets began quietly shifting an entire tank army from this area northward to a more promising bridgehead located at Lyutezh.

flying extremely low, and the Germans could plainly see that many were transports. Stranger still, they had their cabin lights on—some even began training searchlights along the ground. Suddenly, puffy white parachutes appeared, trailing away from the planes.

Thus began a daring Russian effort to enlarge and consolidate bridgeheads by landing thousands of paratroopers—the first large drop ever attempted by the Soviets in wartime. The result was a slaughter. Trying to insert a force at Kolesishche Windmill near Grigorovka, and following that with other attempts near Balyka and the Bukrin bridgehead, the Russian leadership blundered badly. The Soviet 5th Airborne Brigade missed its drop zone by more than twenty miles; the 3d Airborne Brigade dropped 4,575 men without their antitank guns.

Worse, the operation did not come off until after Nehring's corps had made its crossing north of Kanev. Many of the paratroopers dropped directly into territory occupied by heavily armed German units. Though frozen momentarily by the shock of seeing thousands of parachutes opening high overhead, the German troops quickly opened fire with everything they had. Drifting down, caught on tree limbs, the helpless paratroopers made easy targets and were wiped out.

But only forty-eight hours after that Soviet failure came a sudden attack that developed swiftly into one of the major turning points of the war. A twenty-two-man platoon of the 5th Company, 842d Rifle Regiment, commanded by a courageous sergeant named Nefedov, boarded four small fishing boats and landed on the west bank of the Dnieper at the village of Lyutezh, north of Kiev. Dug in on a high bank, the platoon was reduced by German sniper fire to ten men, and Nefedov called desperately for reinforcements. During the next few days, a succession of crossings brought to the west bank two Soviet regiments with field artillery and parts of a heavy mortar regiment. These troops forged a bridgehead around Lyutezh a couple of miles long and a mile deep. Despite heavy fire by units of the German XIII Corps, the Russians held on.

General Vatutin, commander of the Voronezh Front, grabbed at the chance offered by this daring initiative. He and Nikita Khrushchev, a member of his military council, ordered General A. G. Kravchenko, commander of the Fifth Guards Tank Army, to race to the Dnieper bridgehead. This was no easy task because Kravchenko's tanks would not only have to cross the Dnieper but, before that, the Desna River. And the Desna was 1,000 feet wide in this sector. Vatutin pointedly said that bringing up bridging gear and building bridges would take "eight or ten days, but eight days from now will probably be too late." He told Kravchenko, "You've got to find a ford."

Guided by a fisherman to a point where the river's bottom was firm sand, Kravchenko's men wasted no time. The Fifth Guards, he wrote later, "had to turn our tanks into makeshift submarines. All slits, hatches, and covers on the tank hulls and turrets were made watertight and covered with oiled canvas. The tanks then drove off in low gear through the strange corridor."

Once past the Desna, the T-34s moved quickly to the Dnieper, where, on the night of October 5, the Russians used two large barges they found along the banks to ferry sixty tanks across the river. That force kept the German units from overrunning the bridgehead there. Slow at first to exploit this new development, the Soviet high command continued to concentrate its efforts on a breakout farther south, at the bridgehead established near Bukrin. Only after mid-October, when the generals finally concluded that the German cordon around Bukrin was too strong to breach, did they switch the main point of their attack to Lyutezh.

On October 24, showing skill and speed learned from two years of bitter warfare, the Soviets began moving the entire Third Guards Tank Army—shifting more than 300 tanks and self-propelled guns and hundreds of artillery pieces, armored personnel carriers, cars, and trucks over the 120 miles between Bukrin and the crossing at Lyutezh. The Russians replaced the withdrawn tanks and trucks with dummy vehicles, to confound German aerial reconnaissance, and maintained normal radio traffic at the Bukrin bridgehead while enforcing radio silence by the troops on the move.

With three armies, a tank corps, a cavalry corps, and artillery on a massive scale, Vatutin now had forces at Lyutezh far superior to those of the Germans. His Voronezh Front, which was renamed on October 20 the First Ukrainian Front (the Steppe, South-West, and South fronts became, respectively, the Second, Third, and Fourth Ukrainian fronts), was estimated to have a gun or mortar at every ten feet of its line facing the Germans.

The depleted VII and XIII corps of Hoth's Fourth Panzer Army took the brunt of the Russian blows. The most devastating came on November 4

Carrying a wounded comrade in an improvised litter, Soviet partisans wade through the Pripet Marshes north of Kiev. The vast swampland, situated between Army Groups Center and South, was difficult for large armed units to penetrate and thus made an excellent Soviet guerilla base for launching raids against the Germans.

from Rybalko's Third Guards Tank Army, which attacked at night with glaring headlights and shrieking sirens. The Russian armor broke through Hoth's lines north of and in front of Kiev. Threatened with encirclement, Hoth was forced to fall back from the city.

On November 7, Soviet T-34s lumbered down Kiev's main street, and the red flag was raised over the ruins of party headquarters. It was the anniversary of the Bolshevik Revolution—the day Nikita Khrushchev had vowed to liberate the Ukrainian capital. Khrushchev proudly entered the city in a general's uniform. General Rybalko, however, did not pause to bask in glory's light. He pushed on west and south, intent on severing Army Group South's supply lines and communications. The rail yards at Fastov soon fell to Rybalko's tank army, despite a last-ditch defense by Luftwaffe antiaircraft batteries that could only slow him down.

A sign reading "Capture Kiev" urges Soviet troops forward across the Dnieper. German forces were cleared from the Ukrainian capital by November 7, 1943, the anniversary of the Bolshevik Revolution.

Desperate to stop Rybalko, the Germans threw into the lines Lieut. General Adolf von Schell's 25th Panzer Division, a unit that had only recently been cobbled together in Norway and briefly trained in France. Its components had never fought together as a division and were new to the harrowing conditions of the eastern front. The division's best hope was its armor—ninety Panzer IV tanks and forty-five Tigers, about equal in number to Rybalko's T-34s—but most of these tanks had been misdirected to a

Resplendent in his fur-collared greatcoat, Nikita Khrushchev, Ukrainian party chief, military commissar, and future leader of the Soviet Union, comforts a grieving woman after the liberation of Kiev.

German soldiers retreating from Zhitomir, eighty-five miles west of Kiev, glance at the conflagration they have set off. As the Germans withdrew, they devastated entire cities.

depot 120 miles from the fighting. The troops of the 25th had to attack without their armor, suffering crippling losses. When the panzers finally began showing up, General von Schell led them against the Russians holding Fastov again and again, regaining the rail yards but in the end being driven back. The German armor was not strong enough to dislodge the Russians, but their fierce attacks had the effect of preventing Rybalko from completing an envelopment of the entire Army Group South.

While Manstein's forces were throwing everything they could muster against the small but potentially dangerous new bridgehead at Lyutezh in the desperate days of early October, Army Group South faced a far more immediate threat on the lower Dnieper at Zaporozhe. Hitler considered this city to be vital. Its great dam and power station generated electricity for the factories and mines of the entire western Ukraine. As long as German forces were stationed on the eastern bank there, they would remain a threat to the flanks of any Soviet push to the Sea of Azov and the entrance to the Crimea. Assigned to hold Zaporozhe were three panzer divisions from XL Panzer Corps and the infantry divisions of XVII Army Corps, under General Siegfried Henrici. Striving to dislodge Henrici was the Soviet Third Ukrainian Front, with three armies, an air arm, and two tank corps.

Intense bombardment of the German lines kicked off the battle for Zaporozhe on the 10th of October. The struggle between the opposing forces was marked by the repetition of furious advance and retreat—Soviet tanks pushing forward, German infantry with antitank weapons shoving the attackers back, the endless stream of tanks coming again. As the German position deteriorated, a Soviet plane dropped a letter by parachute from General Walter von Seydlitz-Kurzbach, who had been captured by the Soviets at Stalingrad; it was addressed to Lieut. General Erwin Rauch of the 123d Infantry Division. Seydlitz-Kurzbach implored his fellow officer to surrender: "You still remember the days when we were at the Military Academy together. Your division is in a hopeless situation. I have arranged honorable and favorable conditions." A similar overture came from the once-popular Colonel Hans Günther van Hooven, a former panzer commander and, like Seydlitz-Kurzbach, a Russian prisoner. Despite those pleas, no German surrendered. But on the fourth day of the battle, when the dam came under intensive Soviet artillery fire, it became apparent that a German defeat was inevitable.

Henrici, facing the annihilation of his forces, desperately sought permission on October 13 to withdraw from Zaporozhe, but his attempts to communicate with Hitler's headquarters were fruitless: "Still no instructions from Wolfsschanze?" he asked time and time again. "No, Herr General," was always the reply. In fact, the Führer was asleep, and no one dared wake him, particularly with another request from one of his generals for permission to retreat.

With Zaporozhe in flames and Soviet tanks penetrating his lines, Henrici made up his mind to act, permission or not. After retrieving the 16th Panzergrenadier Division and other units on the east bank of the river, Henrici gave his momentous order for the demolition of the railroad bridge and the massive dam. A thunderous blast powered by 580,000 pounds of explosives ripped the dam and powerhouse—although the destruction, it later turned out, was far from complete—and a great wave of water burst through to flood the nearby villages and valley.

After occupying Zaporozhe on the 15th of October, the Soviets drove on to the south and west, toward the Dnieper estuary and the gateway to the Crimea. Eight hundred tanks battered the depleted Sixth Army, whose mission now was to save the vast triangle of land east of the lower Dnieper. That wild steppe swarmed with partisans, who controlled hundreds of villages; the German force had to divert some of its dwindling strength to counter them. In the end, the Sixth Army's task turned out to be impossible. By the third week in October, after bitter and costly fighting, General Hollidt finally had to desert the porous Wotan Line and move westward. Melitopol, a key city on the Sea of Azov, fell to the Russians on the 23d of October.

The Sixth Army's retreat endangered the German position in the Nikopol area—with its reserves of manganese ore—and the entire Crimea. Under increasing pressure, Manstein resumed his dialogue with Hitler. In a meeting of the two at Wolfsschanze on November 7, Hitler insisted that the Nikopol-Crimea region be held, asserting that without its manganese, the German armaments industry would quickly grind to a halt.

Unbeknownst to Hitler, however, armaments minister Albert Speer, prompted by a plea from OKH, had done a study showing that the Reich had enough manganese stocks to continue making high-grade steel for another eleven months, and had released the results to General Zeitzler, the chief of staff. Hitler was beside himself. "You've put me in an intolerable situation," he raged at Speer. "I have just given orders for all available forces to be concentrated for the defense of Nikopol. At last I have a reason to force the army group to fight! And then Zeitzler comes along with your memo. It makes me out a liar! If Nikopol is lost now, it's your fault."

Determined to hang on to Nikopol and keep open the Perekop Isthmus—the land bridge to the Crimea—Hitler at the end of October had placed the defense of the Dnieper bend in the hands of General Ferdinand Schörner, a much-decorated, iron-willed commander of mountain troops who was also a dedicated Nazi. Even Schörner, however, could not overcome the obstacles of overwhelming Soviet strength and a badly bent German line

A section of the 800-yard-long Zaporozhe Dam athwart the southern Dnieper River lies in ruins after the Germans retreated west across it for the last time in October of 1943 and then blew up the span.

German grenadiers, their faces showing the strain of their difficult and dangerous retreat during the waning months of 1943, fall out exhausted for a break in their march westward. While many simply sprawl on the ground, others take the precaution of finding cover.

on the right flank of Army Group South. By Christmas, he too was thinking about a withdrawal.

On January 4, 1944, in a scene both familiar and ever more desperate, Manstein met again with Hitler at the Führer's headquarters. Manstein made clear the perilous situation of Army Group South and urged a pull-back of the forces that remained around the Dnieper bend, even if that meant abandoning the Crimea. After recounting all the old reasons, this time Manstein exceeded even the candor he had shown during earlier meetings: "One thing we must be clear about, my Führer, is that the extremely critical situation we are in now cannot be put down to the enemy's superiority alone. It is also due to the way in which we are led." Hitler's hard stare—"boring into me," wrote Manstein, "as though to force me to my knees"—ended the interview.

As Manstein had predicted, the approaches to the Crimea were soon under Soviet control. The Seventeenth Army was cut off. Manstein's judgment was vindicated, but his cause was lost. The defense of Nikopol and the rest of the German holdings east of the lower Dnieper was taken out of his hands when, on February 2, the Sixth Army was officially transferred from Army Group South to Field Marshal von Kleist's Army Group A.

The tough, experienced troops of Group Schörner—the IV Corps, XXIX Corps, and the XVII Mountain Corps—fought desperately to hold on to this territory. The grim grip of winter added to their woes. Against their Nikopol bridgehead—now shrunk to a shallow arc of land seventy-five miles wide backed up against the river—the Third Ukrainian Front's Eighth Guards and Sixth armies and the Fourth Ukrainian Front's Third Guards and Fifth Shock armies moved steadily ahead in driving snow, despite locally successful German counterattacks. With blizzards pounding and temperatures diving to fifteen degrees below zero, with men suffering and dying, General Schörner in February 1944 faced overwhelming enemy strength. The land to Schörner's rear, a mere six to nine miles of flat, swampy, featureless terrain on the Dnieper, offered little room for maneuver.

Like Henrici at Zaporozhe, Schörner feared that if he waited for a decision from the high command, his troops would be annihilated. Again like Henrici, he made his own decision to withdraw Group Schörner. Professional and proficient, Schörner managed to keep open a narrow corridor between Apostolovo and the Dnieper. By mid-February, his troops had crossed the river. They had escaped the trap—but Nikopol, another of Hitler's too-cherished possessions, was lost, and the last territory east of the Dnieper was gone.

One hundred miles to the north, a similar drama was in its final act. For three months, armored forces such as the Grossdeutschland Division,

In late February 1944, small groups of German troops, dressed in winter gear, move silently through the night in order to slip through the Soviet encirclement around the town of Korsun. About 30,000 Germans were either killed or captured in this stranglehold, known as the Cherkassy pocket.

which had more than the usual complement of tanks, had been dashing from crisis to crisis around Kirovograd, holding off Soviet General Ivan Konev's Second Ukrainian Front. In a virtuoso performance, one heroic sergeant, Sepp Rampel, knocked out eighteen Russian tanks with his Tiger. By January 7, however, the force assigned to defend Kirovograd proper, the 3d Panzer Division, was in danger of being trapped and annihilated by Konev's rapidly advancing forces. On that day, Lieut. General Fritz Bayerlein, formerly Rommel's chief of staff in the North African desert and now commander of the 3d Panzer, inspected the division's front and announced that his troops faced a "hell of a situation."

Bayerlein, like Henrici and Schörner, made the difficult decision. Acting against Hitler's express orders—such action was becoming less unusual as the orders became more and more unrealistic—he broke through the Russian troops circling Kirovograd and escaped, leaving the city to Soviet occupation on January 8.

All along Manstein's endangered front, such episodes were being repeated as the Soviets kept coming. With his ingenuity, Manstein still managed to postpone the inevitable, inflicting heavy losses on the enemy as he did so. But on January 25 and 26, troops of the First and Second Ukrainian fronts broke through the Eighth Army's lines southwest of Kiev and made threatening advances to the south and west. The Fourth Guards Army slashed through the German lines south of the town of Cherkassy, located on the Dnieper about 100 miles downriver from Kiev, and the next day, two corps of the Sixth Tank Army cut a swath through the First Panzer Army front north of the town. The two Soviet forces linked up on January 28, trapping 60,600 troops of the Eighth Army's XLII and XI corps in a pocket that was centered on the town of Korsun, about 30 miles west of Cherkassy.

Manstein assembled a column of panzer divisions, whose tanks—with air support—smashed toward the Cherkassy pocket, as the Germans called it, in an effort to relieve the forces trapped inside. In the process, the panzers destroyed or captured more than 700 Russian tanks along their route. They were unable, however, to break the powerful Soviet ring around Korsun, and several subsequent panzer attacks, despite desperate fighting, also failed to reach the trapped Germans. In the end, somewhere between 30,000 and 32,000 men managed to fight their way out of the pocket.

But the price was high. About 30,000 German troops were killed, wounded, or captured in this latest horror of the eastern front. The 113th Pan-

Destroyed German trucks and armored vehicles suggest the ferocity of the fighting in the Cherkassy pocket as well as the extent of the disaster for the Wehrmacht.

zergrenadier Regiment lost all but 60 of its 600 men. Hundreds of men and horses were drowned attempting to break out of the pocket by crossing an icy stream, the Gniloy Tikich. Most of the German wounded had to be left behind in the frigid mud. Guns and heavy weapons were abandoned. Major General W. Stemmerman, commander of the XI Corps, was killed by tank fire; according to a Russian officer, "his body was laid out on a rough wooden table in a barn, complete with his orders and medals."

The Soviets now seemed unstoppable. In early March, the First Ukrainian Front, commanded now by General Georgy Zhukov after Vatutin was fatally wounded in February by a band of anti-Soviet Ukrainian irregulars, attacked the First and Fourth Panzer armies in the region between the Pripet Marshes and the Carpathian Mountains, near the junction of the prewar borders of Poland, Rumania, and the Soviet Union. Farther south, the city of Uman, the principal base of General Hans Hube's First Panzer Army, fell to Zhukov's forces, which then drove on to the Bug River and beyond, not stopping until they had crossed the Rumanian border, an advance of 250 miles in less than a month.

On March 24, Manstein disobeyed Hitler's orders once again. Hube's First Panzer Army, ordered by Hitler to stand and fight between the Bug and Dniester rivers, was in danger of being surrounded by converging Soviet spearheads of the First and Second Ukrainian fronts. To avoid disaster, Manstein gave permission for the First Panzer to withdraw westward. German troops, making their way through blizzards—which at least kept the Soviet air force grounded—while taking and inflicting heavy losses, finally broke out of the pincers. To Hitler, the action registered as yet another case of disobedience by Manstein.

The following day at the Berghof, the Führer's hideaway in the Bavarian Alps, Hitler and Manstein faced each other in icy anger. To Hitler's accusation that "all that happens is that you are falling back farther and farther," Manstein responded: "You, my Führer, are to be blamed for what has happened. Responsibility for it lies entirely at your door."

On March 30, Hitler abruptly sent his private plane to collect both Manstein and Kleist, commander of Army Group A, and bring them to Berchtesgaden for yet another meeting—as it turned out, their last. After awarding Manstein Swords to his Knight's Cross and making complimentary and conciliatory conversation, the Führer said that the East offered no "further scope" for an officer of his abilities. "I have decided to part company with you and to appoint someone else to the army group. The time for operating is over. What I need now are men who stand firm." Thus ended the career of one of the Reich's most brilliant and dedicated generals. Kleist, who had clashed with Hitler over the need to withdraw Army

Captured German soldiers are paraded through the streets of Leningrad under heavy Soviet guard. After almost three years of brutal siege, the city was finally relieved by the Red Army on January 27, 1944.

Group A from the Crimea, received the same medal and the same dismissal.

With the change of leadership came new designations for the two army groups. Manstein's command was taken over by Field Marshal Walther Model and renamed Army Group North Ukraine; Kleist's Army Group A became Army Group South Ukraine, under General Schörner. In neither case did the changes lessen the perils that the army groups faced.

At the northern end of the front, the German frustrations with Leningrad continued. Hitler's decision in 1941 to capture the city by siege instead of direct assault brought its residents 900 days of starvation, sickness, cold, and death. But under the command of a resolute Ukrainian, General Andrey Zhdanov, the defenders of Leningrad refused to yield.

Now, in the winter of 1943-44, the besieging force, Field Marshal Georg von Küchler's Army Group North, stood in largely the same position it had occupied for the past two years. The Eighteenth Army of General Georg Lindemann held the northern sector of the front. Lindemann's left flank faced the substantial Oranienbaum beachhead on the Gulf of Finland just west of Leningrad, a Soviet salient that Hitler had unaccountably left undisturbed throughout the siege. The Eighteenth Army's center maintained its stalemated stranglehold on the city, lined up against the Leningrad and Volkhov fronts, which outnumbered it three to one in men and artillery, and six to one in tanks, assault guns, and aircraft. The Eighteenth Army's right was anchored on Novgorod and Lake Ilmen. The Sixteenth Army of General Christian Hansen held the southern sector of Army Group North, from Lake Ilmen to the boundary with Army Group Center, located northeast of Vitebsk.

In the closing months of 1943, Eighteenth Army intelligence picked up signs that Soviet forces in the Oranienbaum pocket and on the Leningrad front were being reinforced. A January offensive seemed likely, but it was expected to be of no great intensity. On January 14, a massive Soviet breakout from the Leningrad encirclement burst upon Lindemann with stunning fury. Driving from Oranienbaum, the Second Shock Army fell on the Germans, pushing back two Luftwaffe field divisions, the SS Panzergrenadier Division Nordland, and other Eighteenth Army units. Coordinated with the Oranienbaum breakout was an attack from the Leningrad perimeter by the Soviet Forty-second Army. The Eighteenth's southern flank also came under a pounding, north and south of Novgorod.

In the face of such overwhelming force, Küchler, like Manstein before him, began a retreat. Within five days, the Second Shock Army and the Forty-second Army had made contact, chewing up the divisions caught between them and driving the German siege guns back, out of range of Leningrad. German troops at Novgorod managed to break out of an encirclement there and withdraw to the west, but were forced to leave their wounded behind in the city's ruins.

On January 27, when German commanders all up and down the eastern front were fighting desperate rearguard actions to keep from losing their forces a division or corps at a time, Hitler convened them at a Nazi leadership conference in Königsberg. There, he lectured them on the power of Nazi faith as a key to victory. A few days later, notwithstanding the pep talk, Küchler ordered the Eighteenth Army to draw back to the Luga River.

A furious Hitler replaced him with newly promoted Field Marshal Walther Model, a skilled improviser whose drive even Manstein praised. Despite the change of command, the retreat to the Luga went on—albeit under the rubric of a doctrine, newly minted by Hitler, called *Schild und Schwert* (Shield and Sword). According to this theory, tactical withdrawals were permissible if they were intended as a means of establishing a favorable situation for a counterattack. In practice, the shield portion of the maneuver was carried out far more often than the riposte.

Hardly had Model taken command of Army Group North when his right wing, the Sixteenth Army, came under heavy attack from General Andrey

Soviet ski troops armed with submachine guns prepare an ambush for the Germans of Army Group North. By the end of March 1944, that army group had withdrawn westward to the Panther Line, a stretch of the "east wall" and the last true defensive bastion in the north.

Yeremenko's Second Baltic Front and began to fall back. On February 15, Hitler finally had to agree to the withdrawal of what was left of Army Group North to the Panther Line. The 300-mile-long bulwark, made up of tank obstacles, wire entanglements, and concrete shelters, was formidable; furthermore, a stretch of the line was formed by the natural barriers of Lake Peipus and Lake Pakov. Once they were safely behind the Panther Line on March 1, the Germans were able to hold their position for several months—until the relentless Soviet push overcame even that obstacle, and the German retreat began once more.

From the spring of 1943 to the spring of 1944, the German situation on the eastern front had gone from tenable to disastrous. The year had begun with eleven German armies holding a serpentine front from the Gulf of Finland to the Sea of Azov, some of its penetrations deep enough to threaten Moscow. By March 1944, the front had been rolled back in some places nearly 400 miles to the west. Soviet troops had reached the gates of Poland.

The cost to the Russians had been horrendous: Five million men had been lost in two and a half years of fighting. Soviet numerical superiority, however, was ever growing. At the beginning of 1944, seven million Russians were under arms. Over the entire front, from the Arctic to the Black Sea, Stalin possessed the enormous aligned strength of fifty-eight armies. Facing every German were swelling numbers of soldiers of the Red Army, thirsting for revenge against those who had caused their people so much agony and grief. The stage was set for a German calamity, which began to unfold in the Crimea. ✚

The Grueling Retreat of the 197th

Among the German troops engaged in the general retreat through the Soviet Union was the 197th Infantry Division of the Third Panzer Army. As part of Army Group Center, the division had helped spearhead Germany's bold assault on the Soviets in June 1941 and had fought its way to the gates of Moscow. But that was as far as it got. Beset by vicious Red Army counterattacks and worn down by bone-chilling winters that froze machines as well as men, the soldiers of the 197th soon found themselves in full retreat. In 1942 and 1943, they paused long enough to fight defensive battles west of Moscow near the Belorussian cities of Smolensk and Orsha. Harassed by partisans behind the lines and dogged by Soviets at their heels, the division also had to contend with muddy roads in the spring and frozen roads in the winter, conditions that made the journey difficult for tracked vehicles and next to impossible for the foot soldiers and their horse-drawn supply wagons.

Recording the 197th's retreat was its unofficial photographer, Carl Henrich, whose pictorial journal appears on these pages. Henrich joined the unit as a radio operator in 1941 and stayed with it until it was torn apart at Vitebsk during the Soviet army's massive summer offensive in 1944. The division suffered such heavy losses that it ceased to exist as a fighting unit; its survivors were reassigned to other German divisions, which continued the fighting withdrawal through Lithuania and East Prussia. By the summer of 1945, only 7,000 of the division's 17,000 original soldiers had made it back to Germany. Among the survivors was Henrich, who cherished memories of his division long after the war. One of his most poignant was that of the death of his commanding officer. "Our general walked by the trench we were sitting in," Henrich recalled. "He wished us all a good night in spite of everything. A curious expression came on his face as if it was goodbye forever. Later, bombs destroyed his car, and he burned in it. He was buried right then and there."

Private Carl Henrich of the 197th Infantry Division adjusts the camera he used to chronicle the retreat of his unit. Henrich's superiors allowed him to indulge his hobby and snap pictures in rare spare moments.

During a skirmish on a barren plain, troops of the 197th Infantry Division use the bodies of fallen Red Army soldiers as cover. The Russian steppe offered little natural protection; men found whatever they could.

Using an abandoned cabin for cover, two Germans with an antitank gun watch for enemy troops as a village burns in the distance. In spite of the rapidly advancing Soviets, German forces managed to reduce countless Russian towns and villages to cinders.

Dressed in warm winter uniforms, soldiers of the 197th prepare to break camp and resume their march west. In 1941, the division struggled through its first Soviet winter with only threadbare summer outfits. By the following winter, however, the majority of the German troops on the eastern front were properly garbed.

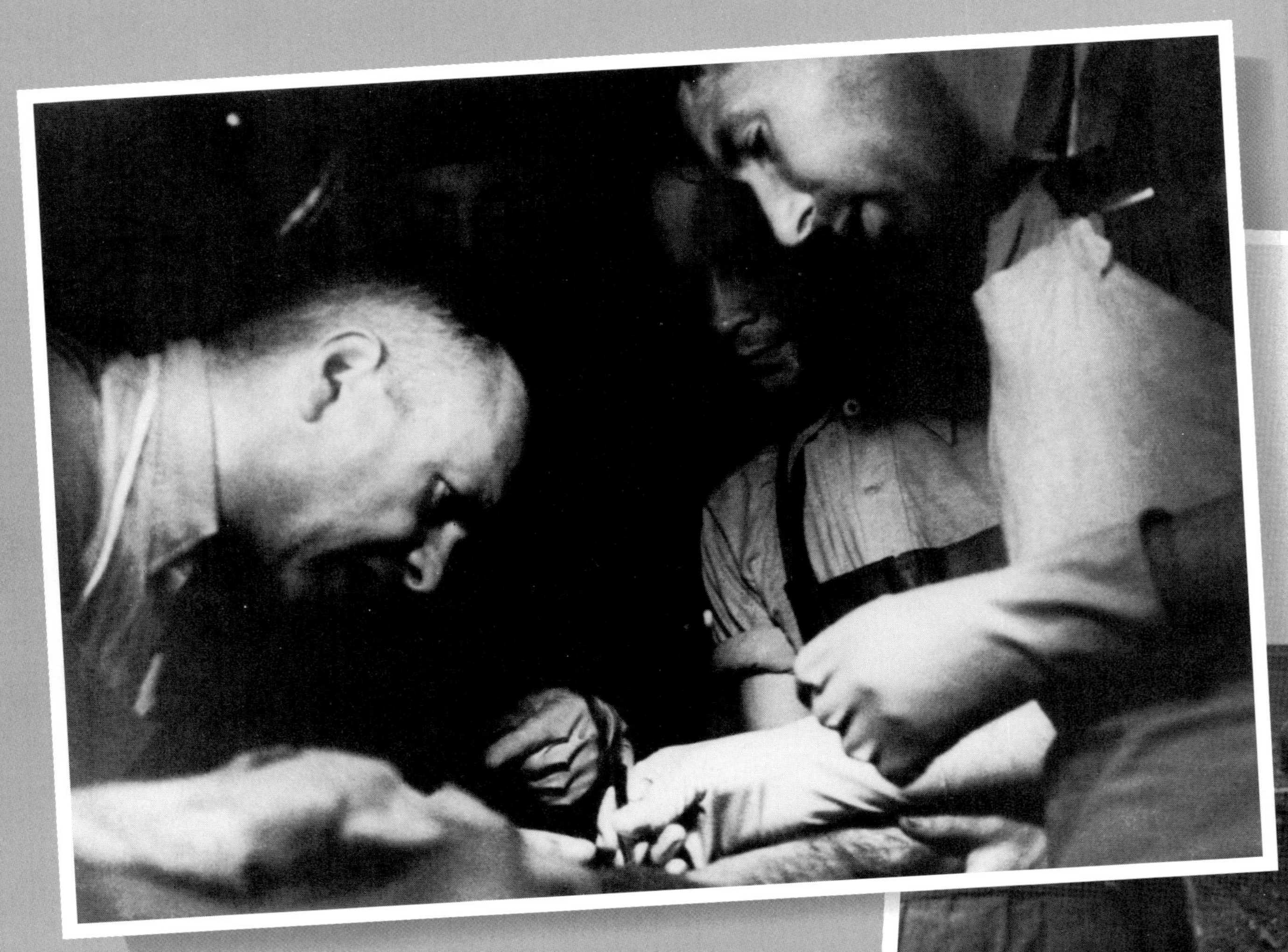

Making the best of crude facilities, division surgeons perform an operation in a front-line bunker near Olenino, 150 miles west of Moscow. According to Henrich, "Patients were anesthetized with rags drenched in chloroform while their shredded limbs were removed."

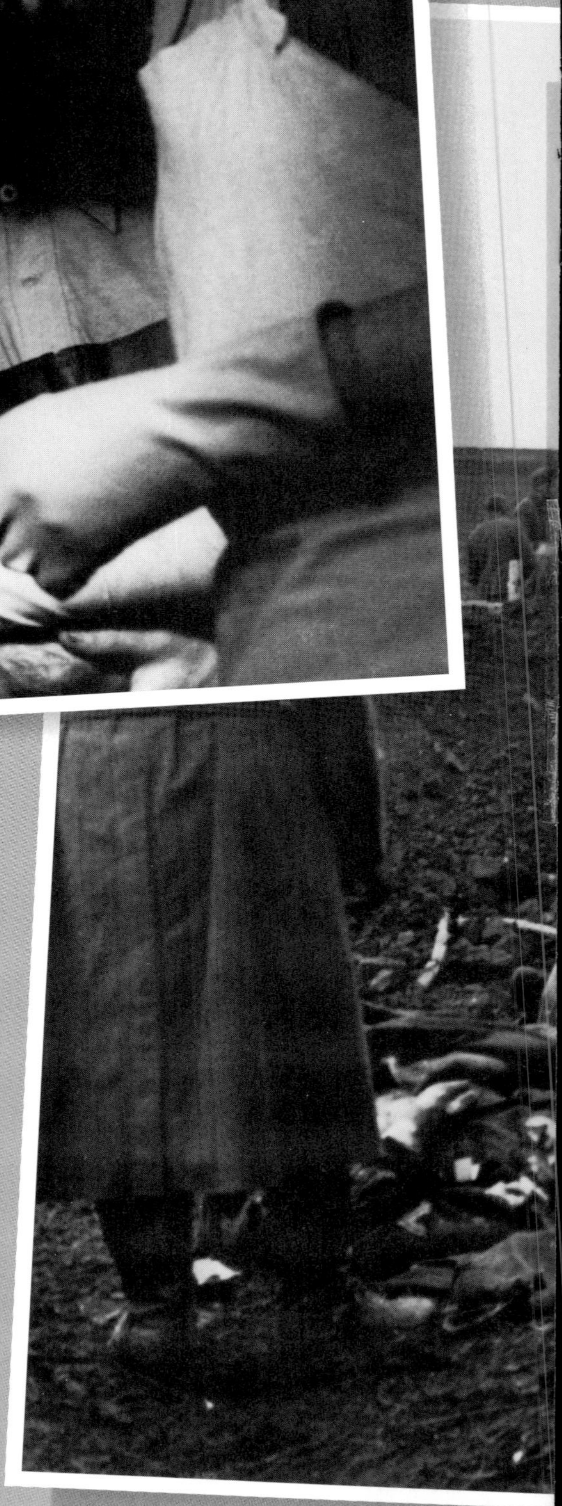

At a Russian cemetery, crude crosses mark the graves of German dead while a row of corpses awaits burial. Henrich remembered, "During the winter, the frozen ground had to be blasted open. If a snowstorm developed, many of our dead remained hidden from us under a blanket of snow and were listed as missing." As casualties rose, bodies were hastily buried in mass graves in the countryside.

Men from the 197th Division withdraw after torching a village. Of the incident, Henrich recalled, "The enemy artillery fire became stronger, causing the horses that were pulling our wagons to rear up in fright. Alongside a house wall, a soldier was bleeding to death, and next to him a dead comrade."

Soldiers prepare to fire harmless grenades that released safe-conduct passes upon impact. The Germans hoped that the Soviet troops would choose captivity over the hazards of fighting and use the passes to become prisoners of war.

Russian farmers smile gamely for the camera after joining forces with the 197th to battle partisans. Many Russians gladly accepted rewards of food, weapons, and ammunition from the Germans in exchange for fighting against the insurgents.

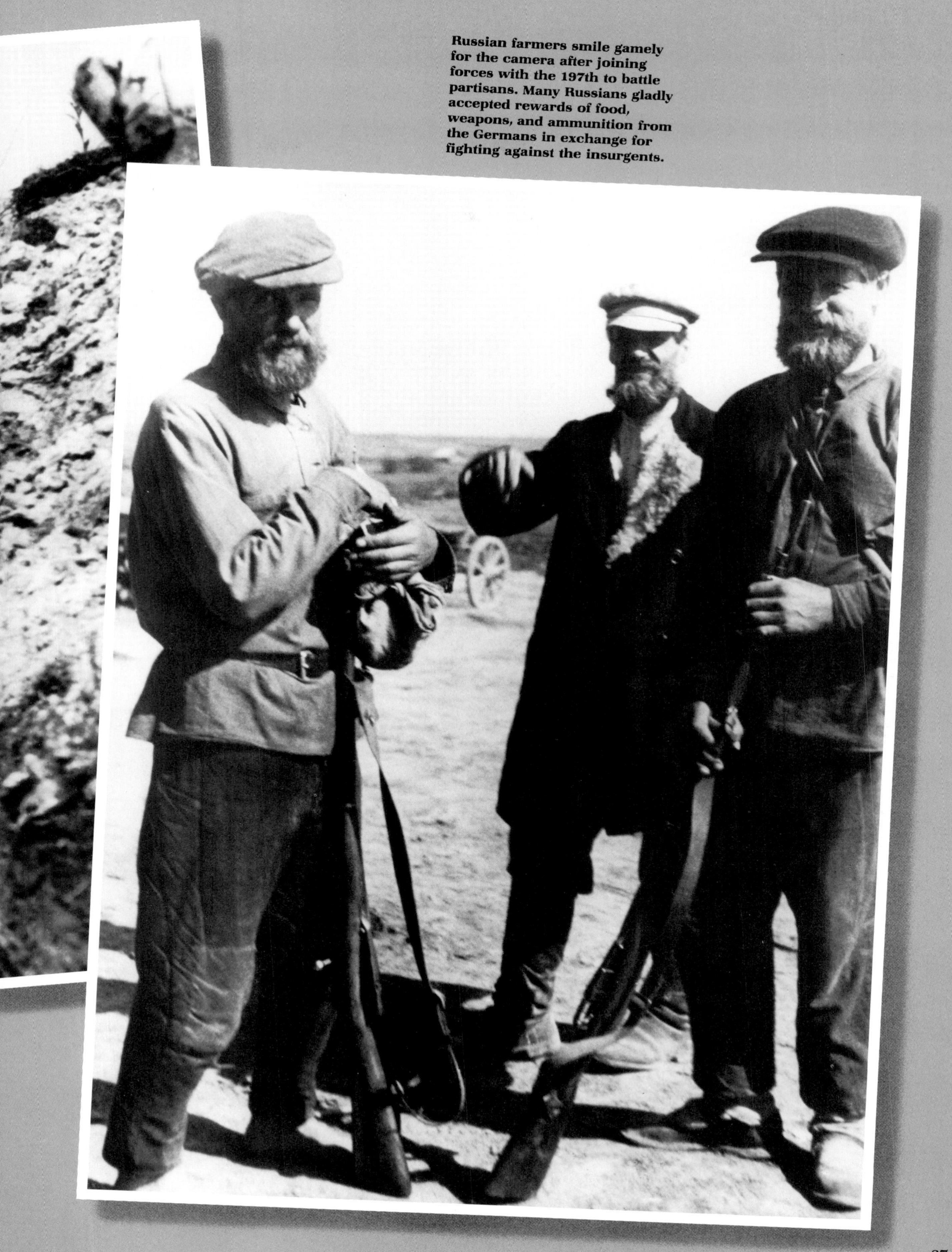

A soldier separated from the 197th in June 1944 during fighting at Vitebsk shows the compass he used to find his way back to German lines. Fearing death at the hands of the Red Army or partisans, he shed his uniform during his weeks-long trek and donned castoff clothing he found in a barn. Henrich related that many such soldiers returned wearing "any sort of mufti they could find, anything but a German uniform."

Russian refugees carrying their possessions flee from Vitebsk with troops of the 197th. The Germans forcibly evacuated many Russians to deprive the advancing Soviet army of manpower. But other refugees, fearing their own undisciplined army more than the Germans, joined the retreat willingly.

Ostrowno
II. Kp.

THREE

The Collapse in the Center

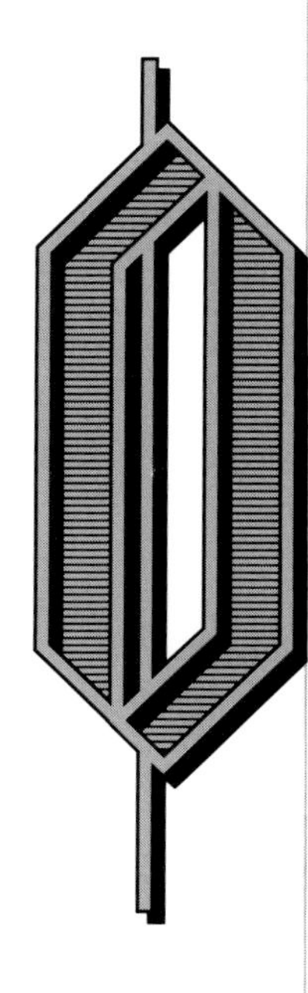

ne day in early June 1944, the quiet skies over the front lines of Army Group Center were disturbed by the sputter of a "sewing machine," a slow, rickety Soviet reconnaissance aircraft. Alert German flak gunners shot the wayward plane down, and a Soviet air staff officer was pulled from the wreckage. In his possession, interrogators found handwritten papers that enabled them to draw clear conclusions about where the expected Russian summer offensive was going to take place.

At a stroke, the Germans had acquired information that might enable them to reverse their declining fortunes on the eastern front. But incredibly, Adolf Hitler squandered the opportunity. Hitler was convinced that Stalin would aim his attack at the Wehrmacht's strength, driving against the heavily reinforced German position south of Army Group Center.

Contrary intelligence—the remarkable papers taken from the Soviet airman, as well as information from other sources—was dismissed by Hitler as irrelevant, since it did not fit into his notion of enemy intentions. Thus, as the ever-stronger, more confident Soviets made ready to expel the invader from their homeland, the flagging German army was increasingly forced to struggle with the obsessions of its Führer just to save itself from destruction. The baneful weight of Hitler's errors was never more costly to his army than it would be in the momentous battles on the eastern front in the summer of 1944.

The spring muds of that year, which brought to a halt the huge Soviet offensive in the south Ukraine in early April, had come none too soon for the retreating Wehrmacht. By now, the Reich, despite Hitler's obduracy on the subject of giving up ground, had lost almost all the Soviet territory it had conquered since the start of Operation Barbarossa and had suffered more than two million casualties as well.

In only two places did the Germans still cling to significant portions of the Soviet homeland. Along the center of the German line, an enormous salient bulged eastward to the Dnieper River and beyond, embracing virtually the whole of Belorussia, a low-lying expanse of farm, forest, and swamp between the Baltic States and the Ukraine. The entire sector, with

During Operation Bagration, the Soviet army's unstoppable offensive against Army Group Center in Belorussia in the summer of 1944, a German platoon leader wounded by an exploding shell is carried from a field hospital by compatriots, one of whom has a head injury. Hitler's insistence on holding Soviet territory in the face of overwhelming odds resulted in high German casualties.

its 660-mile front, belonged for the moment to Army Group Center, which had come under the command of Field Marshal Ernst Busch the previous October, after Field Marshal Günther Hans von Kluge was seriously injured in a traffic accident.

The other region still in German hands was the Crimean peninsula. Here, the Seventeenth Army maintained a precarious foothold in the shadow of a relentless Soviet threat. The previous autumn, Russian forces had surged past the Perekop Isthmus, the sole land link between the Crimea and the mainland, severing the Germans on the peninsula from the rest of Army Group South Ukraine. Then, advance units of the Soviet Fourth Ukrainian Front had skirted the German blocking position athwart the Perekop to cross the Sivash—also known as the Putrid Sea—a ragged-edged, stagnant lagoon lapping the isthmus's eastern shore, and had established several small beachheads on the Crimean north coast. At about the same time, forces from General Andrey Yeremenko's Independent Maritime Army (formerly the North Caucasus Front) had leaped the Kerch Strait from the Kuban peninsula to set up another beachhead on the Crimea's eastern tip. The Seventeenth Army was being measured for a knockout punch.

The army's commander, General Erwin Jaenecke, had long anticipated the approaching danger and had drawn up plans to evacuate his troops. Predictably, Hitler said no. The Führer believed, with some justification, that the Crimea was vital for maintaining a protective air umbrella over German naval operations in the Black Sea and over the Balkans, particularly the Ploesti oil fields. Furthermore, he claimed, a retreat would upset the political balance, perhaps tipping neutral Turkey into the enemy camp. "There are two things I need for the war above everything else: Rumanian oil and Turkish chrome ore," he liked to explain. "Both will be lost if I abandon the Crimea."

So the Seventeenth Army stayed put. Its 150,000 combat troops, consisting of six German and seven Rumanian divisions, all supported by a Luftwaffe fighter corps, dug in for the winter. Ample supplies arrived by naval convoy, up to 50,000 tons a month. A deceptive sense of well-being in the face of impending disaster settled briefly on the army, bringing an air of unreality to the command. "The Crimea is like an island well outside the breaking surf," wrote Captain Hans Ruprecht Hensel of the operations staff. Engineer companies were put to work beautifying officers' billets, rebuilding interiors in traditional German peasant style.

But the massing of Soviet forces could not be ignored. Three Russian armies had gathered on the mainland approaches—some 470,000 troops in all, along with 560 tanks and self-propelled guns and 1,200 aircraft. Jaenecke strengthened his defenses, stringing a double tier of trenches, minefields, and barbed-wire entanglements across the Perekop Isthmus. He laid out a fallback position, called the Gneisenau Line, less than thirty miles in front of the bastion of Sevastopol, on the southern tip of the peninsula. Notwithstanding Hitler's views, he also drew up a new contingency plan, Operation Eagle, which called for a phased withdrawal of all his forces to Sevastopol and their subsequent evacuation by sea. The withdrawal would take a week, he estimated, and the city itself could be held for an additional three weeks, allowing just enough time to pull out the last remaining troops.

In early April, the new commander of Army Group South Ukraine, General Ferdinand Schörner, arrived on a whirlwind inspection tour of the Crimean defenses. Schörner, a military leader after Hitler's own heart—ruthless, overbearing, and aggressive—reported back what Hitler wanted to hear. The Crimea, he told the army high command on April 7, could be held "for a long time."

Few predictions have been so quickly proved wrong. The very next morning, the Soviets launched their assault, with two armies of the Fourth Ukrainian Front under General Fyodor Tolbukhin pouring down the Perekop Isthmus and across the Sivash. The defenders, heavily outnumbered, clung to their positions on the isthmus for twenty-four hours; then, the line collapsed. The second blow came from the east, as the Independent Maritime Army broke from its beachhead and surged westward along the Kerch Peninsula. So weakly manned were the German defenses here that retreating artillery units barely had time to disable their guns to keep them from falling intact into enemy hands.

The Germans withdrew to the arc of trenches that made up the Gneisenau Line. Schörner had estimated that the line might be held for as long as four weeks. But there was no stopping the Russians as they swept across the open plain, twenty-seven divisions strong. They breached the line on April 12; four days later, the last of the German rearguard units staggered into Sevastopol, the Russians close at their heels.

By now, even the German high command understood that the Crimea was lost. Schörner, in an abrupt reversal, began pressing Hitler to authorize the immediate pullout of all Seventeenth Army troops. On his own authority, Schörner had already arranged for a naval convoy to ferry out service units, some of the Rumanian divisions, and the increasing numbers of wounded. But Hitler would not listen. The same day as the Russian breakthrough at the Gneisenau Line, he issued a decree: "Sevastopol will be defended indefinitely. No fighting troops will be evacuated."

The order amounted to a death sentence. Casualties had severely depleted the Seventeenth Army, so that by April 18, its strength was down to

A stoic Soviet soldier advances over a dead German in this 1943 poster that reads "Rid Our Land of Hitlerite Scum." Such posters aimed to stiffen the resolve of the Russians to defeat Germany.

Their hands raised in surrender, three German soldiers in Sevastopol march compliantly into captivity under the watchful eye of a Russian soldier *(right)*.

An aerial photograph shows a ruined Sevastopol *(below)* after the Soviets recaptured the city in May 1944. The Germans destroyed much of the Crimean port when they seized it in 1942.

121,433 soldiers. Of these, the number of trained combat troops amounted to only about 25,000—the equivalent of five regiments. Vital equipment was in desperately short supply. The old Soviet defense system of forts and bunkers had fallen into ruin. Beyond the ridges, regrouping for attack, lay the undiminished Russian force.

Schörner flew to Hitler's command post at the Berghof, hoping the Führer would change his mind and permit a total evacuation. The answer was foreseeable. Then Jaenecke, summoned for consultations, protested openly when ample reinforcements promised by Hitler turned out to be four battalions of green recruits. Hitler fired him and named General Karl Allmendinger, the V Corps commander, in his place.

The Soviet assault on Sevastopol began on May 5, at 9:30 a.m., as five rifle divisions charged the city's northern perimeter. The relatively easy slope of the land in this sector made it the most logical avenue of attack, and the Germans concentrated their defensive forces here—all to no purpose, for two days later, the Russians unleashed a massive artillery barrage against weaker German positions in the east and south and then stormed in with two full armies. By nightfall, they had smashed through the defenses in several places and had captured the strategic Sapun Heights, which overlooked the entire battlefield. The next morning, Soviet units were fighting their way into the city.

Hitler finally faced up to reality. At Schörner's request, on the evening of May 8, he ordered the final evacuation of Sevastopol. Most noncombatant personnel had already been ferried out. The remaining troops—64,700 men—pulled back to a fortified position on nearby Cape Khersones, the westernmost point of land in the Crimea, to await the ships that would carry them to Rumania and safety.

For the next day and a half, the survivors hunkered down on the Kher-

At Cape Khersones, a promontory west of Sevastopol, helmets and rifles abandoned by Hitler's Crimean forces bear witness to the Soviet victory on the peninsula. When Russian troops entered Sevastopol on May 9, some 65,000 Germans fled to the cape, where they eventually were forced to surrender after waiting in vain for rescue.

sones beachhead, fending off wave after wave of enemy ground assaults, while 660-pound shells from Soviet heavy guns rained down on them and Soviet attack planes raked their positions. On May 9, with the Khersones airstrip badly pocked with shell holes, the last Luftwaffe fighters took off for Rumania, ending any prospect of air cover for the rescue ships.

And where were the ships? A pair of naval transports, the *Totila* and the *Teja,* appeared off Khersones in the predawn hours of May 10, and what happened next gave a foretaste of disasters to come. To avoid Soviet artillery, the transports hove to several miles offshore while ferries brought out the soldiers—4,000 for the *Totila,* 5,000 for the *Teja.* Near sunup, as the two ships swung back toward Rumania, Soviet planes struck the crowded *Totila* with three bombs, setting the vessel ablaze. A few hours later, it sank. A Soviet torpedo plane scored a hit on the *Teja,* and it, too, plunged to the bottom. A few hundred men were plucked from the water by rescue craft; others swam back to shore—total losses: 8,000 lives.

A series of misfortunes also beset the main convoys that steamed toward Khersones. A gale blew up in the Black Sea, delaying the timetable by one day. About the time the ships finally arrived off the coast, on the night of May 11, radio communications broke down between the command ship and the rest of the fleet, making it impossible to coordinate landings. Worse yet, many of the ships simply could not find their way to shore. Soviet shelling had set off a series of smoke drums installed over the previous months as part of the shoreline defense system, and most landing points were socked in behind a foglike chemical vapor.

A few vessels got through the smoke that night and, under cover of darkness, rescued somewhat more than half the remaining troops. But as dawn broke, the convoy headed out to sea with many ships still empty. Some 26,700 soldiers were left on the beach either to be killed in a hopeless battle or to end their days in Russian prison camps. In thirty-five days of fighting, the defense of the Crimea had cost roughly 100,000 German and Rumanian lives; the Seventeenth Army had ceased to exist.

In contrast to the catastrophe in the Crimea, the situation of Army Group Center, some 600 miles to the north in Belorussia, appeared secure. After the debacle at Kursk the previous summer and the army group's subsequent withdrawal to the Dnieper's upper reaches, Busch's front line had scarcely budged. On the left, anchored by the Third Panzer Army, it reached out to encompass the fortified city of Vitebsk, less than 300 miles from Moscow. It then swung south in a broad arc whose center consisted of an eighty-mile-wide bridgehead on the eastern bank of the Dnieper, occupied by the Fourth Army. From the right end of this arc, the line angled back west again toward a Dnieper tributary, the Pripet, across lowland terrain held by the Ninth Army.

Here, the front all but vanished, swallowed up by the vast Pripet Marshes, a peat bog roughly the size of Belgium that straddles the border between Belorussia and the Ukraine. Except for a few widely separated east-west roads and tracks, the marshes under most circumstances were impassable; no sizable enemy force could be expected to move through them to assault the right flank of Army Group Center from the south. The Second Army, a mixture of German and Hungarian divisions, manned this sector, extending westward up the Pripet for 250 miles to Kovel to form a link with Army Group North Ukraine.

Army Group Center's territory was immense, roughly a quarter-million square miles. To hold it, Busch could command as much manpower as any general on the eastern front: forty-two infantry divisions, six panzer and panzergrenadier divisions, five *Sicherheit* (Security) divisions—normally equipped and responsible for rear-area stability and antipartisan activity—and three independent brigades, for a total force of nearly 700,000 troops. Given the length of the front, however, each line division would have to defend a fifteen-mile stretch, almost four times the accepted optimum. But no one believed a major defense would be needed here, at least not for now.

The Russians were certainly expected to launch a summer offensive, and even as the skies warmed and the mud dried, the Wehrmacht was preparing to meet it. All the Germans' attention was focused south, toward Galicia, the territory that lies between the Pripet Marshes and the Carpathian Mountains in the northwest corner of the Ukraine. An assault through Galicia could have disastrous consequences for them. The Soviets could follow it by striking south toward the Balkans in the hope of capturing that area's strategic oil reserves. Or they might turn north, thrusting deep into Poland and rolling onward through open country in a massive sweep toward Warsaw and beyond until they reached East Prussia and the Baltic coast, only 280 miles away.

That was what Hitler expected; a flanking offensive through Galicia was just the kind of bold, decisive gamble he would have taken. To guard against it, he stripped Army Group Center of the LVI Panzer Corps and transferred it to Field Marshal Walther Model's Army Group North Ukraine. At a stroke, Busch lost 15 percent of his divisions, one-third of his heavy artillery, half of his tank destroyers, and 88 percent of his tanks. A slight reduction in his overall perimeter—part of the front covered by the departing corps was transferred with it to Model's command—in no way made up for the removal of men and matériel. With nearly all his remaining combat troops dug in along the line, Busch was left with a reserve of only two infantry divisions capable of responding to an enemy breakthrough.

Busch submitted without complaint to Hitler's raid on his forces, although he did fly to the Führer's headquarters to suggest that his front be further shortened by a strategic withdrawal to more easily defended terrain to the west. The response was cold contempt. Every foot of ground must be held, Hitler declared. Even minor adjustments rearward for tactical reasons—the kind of mobile defense that every general on the eastern front was urging—would not be permitted.

This mandate applied most particularly to a series of towns just behind the front line. In March, Hitler had issued a decree designating a number of major supply and communications centers as fortress cities, which would be reinforced and defended to the last man. In the event of a Soviet breakthrough, the fortress cities would presumably tie down the enemy forces that paused to subdue them; they would also serve as rallying points for future counterattacks.

Five such positions came under Army Group Center's command—Slutsk, Bobruisk, Mogilev, Orsha, and Vitebsk—as well as a sixth, Polotsk, just inside the territory of Army Group North. Hitler ordered a full division devoted to the defense of each, with the exception of Vitebsk, which was assigned four divisions. The result was that even fewer troops were available to hold the front line.

Another problem for Busch was the heavy incidence of sabotage along his supply and communications lines. Ever since the Wehrmacht's triumphant gallop through Belorussia on its way to Moscow in 1941, bands of

Three years to the day Hitler launched Operation Barbarossa, the Soviet army, on June 22, 1944, began its offensive in Belorussia against Germany's Army Group Center, 500,000 troops under the command of Field Marshal Ernst Busch. The Red Army amassed 1.2 million men with more than 4,000 tanks supported by 6,000 aircraft. Attacking toward the German headquarters city of Minsk, the Russians advanced ninety-five miles in five days, destroying three German divisions and inflicting more than 200,000 casualties. By mid-July, the Germans had been pushed back into Poland at high cost. The Ninth Army, at Bobruisk and Minsk alone, suffered more than 75,000 losses. An invigorated Red Army now launched its attack on Army Group North. By August 1, the Soviets had reached the Gulf of Riga, effectively cutting off Army Group North. By mid-month, the Russians were poised on the Vistula River.

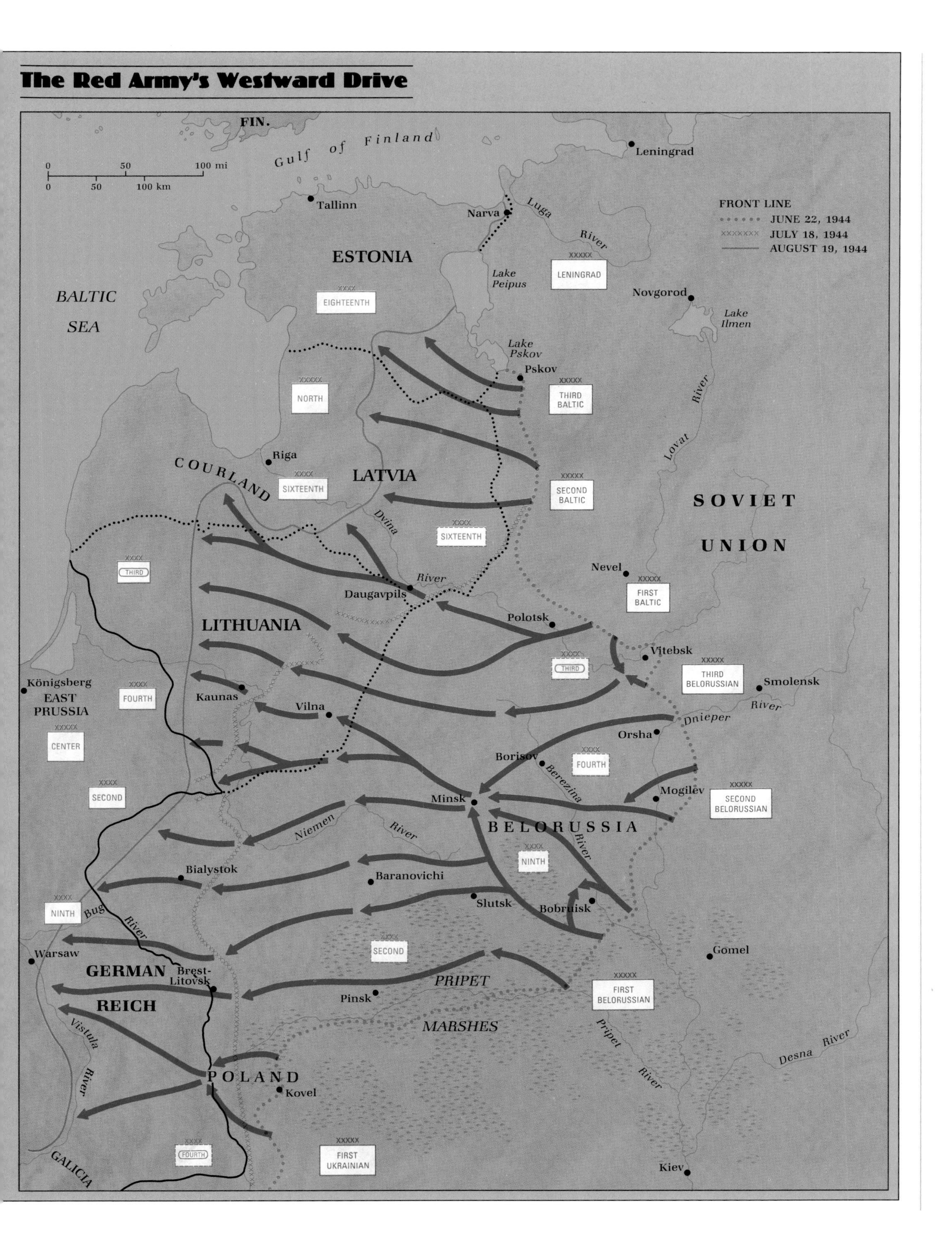
The Red Army's Westward Drive
FRONT LINE
JUNE 22, 1944
JULY 18, 1944
AUGUST 19, 1944
0 50 100 mi
0 50 100 km
FIN.
Gulf of Finland
Leningrad
Tallinn
Narva
Luga River
ESTONIA
LENINGRAD
Lake Peipus
Novgorod
Lake Ilmen
BALTIC SEA
EIGHTEENTH
Lake Pskov
Pskov
NORTH
THIRD BALTIC
Lovat River
Riga
COURLAND
SIXTEENTH
LATVIA
SECOND BALTIC
SOVIET UNION
Dvina River
SIXTEENTH
THIRD
Daugavpils
Nevel
FIRST BALTIC
Polotsk
LITHUANIA
Vitebsk
THIRD
THIRD BELORUSSIAN
Smolensk
Königsberg
EAST PRUSSIA
FOURTH
Kaunas
Vilna
Dnieper River
Orsha
CENTER
Borisov
FOURTH
Berezina River
SECOND
Minsk
Mogilev
SECOND BELORUSSIAN
Niemen River
BELORUSSIA
NINTH
Bialystok
Baranovichi
NINTH
Bug River
Slutsk
Bobruisk
Warsaw
SECOND
Gomel
GERMAN REICH
Brest-Litovsk
PRIPET MARSHES
Pinsk
FIRST BELORUSSIAN
Vistula River
Pripet River
Desna River
POLAND
Kovel
FOURTH
FIRST UKRAINIAN
GALICIA
Kiev

Soviet resistance fighters had been gathering in the region's forests and byways. Some were Red Army soldiers who had become separated from their units during the fighting and were stranded behind the German lines. They were soon joined by government workers and Communist party officials hiding from mobile Nazi killing units out to exterminate them. By the summer of 1943, partisan strength in Belorussia had swelled to some 200,000 fighting men and women. Rail lines, roadways, telephone cables, supply dumps—all were targets of their hit-and-run attacks.

German reprisals were swift and savage but not always effective. Sicherheit squads rounded up and shot peasants and villagers merely suspected of partisan sympathies, a practice that had the contrary effect of driving more recruits into the partisan ranks. Entire German divisions went on retaliatory sweeps through partisan strongholds. Still, the raids continued.

Soldiers on maneuver in partisan territory were at risk from every quarter. Any firm ground in a marshy area could well be seeded with small wooden mines that were imperceptible to metal detectors but capable of blowing off a foot. At any moment, a well-aimed rifle shot might erupt from a nearby thicket. "The worst things in Russia," one trooper wrote home, "are lice and snipers."

Intimidating though they were, the partisans never fully succeeded in closing off Army Group Center's lifeline of supplies and equipment. All through the winter and into the spring of 1944, the trains continued to run. Then, suddenly, the attacks intensified. On the night of June 19, explosions erupted along the tracks from one end of Belorussia to the other, more than 10,500 detonations in all. Rails were twisted, embankments crumbled, phone cables cut, freight cars smashed, and for the next twenty-four hours, not a single train was able to move. During the following three days, more explosions demolished 147 trains, by partisan count. Clearly, a major enemy action of some sort was about to occur.

Along Army Group Center's front line, other indications of stepped-up Soviet activity were all too apparent. For nearly a week, army group field intelligence had been detecting a massive increase in enemy strength, including hundreds of new artillery batteries, battalion-size tank units, and entire infantry divisions. Firefights broke out all along the front, as if the enemy were probing the strength of German defenses.

The army high command back in Germany received these reports with surprising composure. Soviet attacks against Army Group Center were only to be expected, the general staff believed, as a diversionary tactic meant to shift attention from the main offensive—which would take place in the south. The attacks, the Germans reasoned, were supposed to pin down Busch's troops, making them unavailable for the defense of Galicia. Fur-

At War with the Partisans

German soldiers post a roadside sign warning of partisans and ordering drivers to form multivehicle convoys for safety.

As Army Group Center battled the Red Army in the spring of 1944, it was hounded from the rear by a second enemy, Soviet partisans. Such guerrillas had plagued Hitler's army since its 1941 invasion, and by 1943, perhaps 200,000 irregular fighters roved through occupied Russia. The partisans were especially active in Belorussia, where dense forests and swamps provided ideal cover. Using weapons and explosives from abandoned Soviet ammunition dumps and later from Red Air Force drops, ragtag bands of peasants, Communists, and Red Army stragglers blew up trains and attacked truck convoys on the few railroads and highways spanning the region. The sabotage disrupted the flow of supplies from German-held territory and kept troops tied down in the rear at a time when the Wehrmacht desperately needed reinforcements at the front.

Early in the war, these forays were sporadic, as separate bands roamed the region choosing targets that were safe rather than strategically valuable. In time, however, the Red Army began to arm the partisans and slip officers behind the German lines to train them and to coordinate their attacks with those of Soviet army units. German military leaders dismissed early partisan attacks as a passing phenomenon, but the disciplined assaults planned by the Red Army were more than the ill-equipped and understaffed German rear-area units could handle. In an effort to stop the partisans, the Germans turned to terror. Acting on longstanding orders, the Germans began to execute as many as 100 Soviet civilians for every German soldier killed by the partisans. But the terror tactics failed to subdue the movement. Russian peasants, who had been largely indifferent to the war, became alienated by these reprisals and began to join the partisans. The harassment continued, slowing the German withdrawal and devastating the morale of an already drained and deflated army.

Derailed by a partisan bomb, a German supply train *(left)* lies broken on an embankment near Kursk. In just one month in 1944, partisan guerillas set off explosions that damaged 237 locomotives and 824 railroad cars.

Weapons at the ready, a German security unit patrols a rail line in the Ukraine. In order to deprive the partisans of protective cover, the Germans routinely cut back the woods and underbrush near railroad tracks. The irregulars responded by planting mines under cover of darkness.

German soldiers push a disabled truck away from a burning building during a partisan raid. Not knowing when or where the next assault would occur strained the nerves of war-weary German soldiers. "On Sunday, a car blew up by the officers' club," a soldier wrote home. "Many Germans have been shot in the streets from behind corners. I'm cracking up."

A German security patrol attacks a Russian dwelling and drives out a suspected partisan *(left)*. Since guerrillas often launched ambushes from barns and peasant houses, special antipartisan units preceded German supply convoys, searching buildings along the route and questioning occupants.

In Minsk, suspected partisans executed by German troops hang from a makeshift gallows. Around the neck of one is a sign in German and Russian that reads, "We are partisans and have killed German soldiers." Instead of discouraging partisan activity, the killing of often-innocent men, women, and even children only drove Russians into the ranks of the irregulars.

thermore, as Field Marshal Wilhelm Keitel, chief of the armed forces high command, pointed out in a briefing on June 20, Stalin would never move until the Allies had widened their foothold in France, where they had made a massive landing on the beaches of Normandy two weeks earlier.

The view from the front was considerably more pessimistic. On June 22, General Hans Jordan noted in his command's war diary: "Ninth Army stands on the eve of another great battle, unpredictable in extent and duration. The enemy has completed an assembly on the very greatest scale." Jordan went on to record that his army was likely to have a difficult time confronting it, given Hitler's orders for a rigid defense. He looked to the battle ahead, he said, "with bitterness."

But as Jordan would shortly learn, the battle had already begun. That very morning, which was by no coincidence the third anniversary of the starting date of Hitler's war against the Soviet Union, Russian troops had charged across the line held by the Third Panzer Army, on the army group's left flank, and were rolling up the German defenses at blitzkrieg speed.

Plans for a major campaign into Belorussia had been forming on Stalin's desk for several months. The German salient posed a worrisome obstacle for the Soviets, since it menaced with a possible flanking attack any further advance from the south into Poland. At the same time, with its straggly perimeter and exposed flanks, the bulge presented a tempting target. Stalin handed over the details of planning and execution to his two top commanders, Generals Alexander Vasilevsky and Georgy Zhukov, and by mid-May, the operational scheme was complete.

Four Soviet formations would charge into the salient in a series of coordinated attacks over a forty-eight-hour period. In the north, under Vasilevsky's command, the First Baltic Front and the Third Belorussian Front would kick off the offensive by assaulting the German left flank along the Dvina River, striking south from above Polotsk and east from just below Vitebsk, to envelop the Third Panzer Army. Next, the Second Belorussian Front, under Zhukov, would go into action in the center, hitting the German Fourth Army bridgehead on the Dnieper, driving the defenders back across the river, and gobbling up the fortress city of Mogilev. During the third phase of the offensive, the First Belorussian Front, also under Zhukov, would swing up from the south, near the edge of the Pripet Marshes, to encircle the German Ninth Army in a two-pronged assault on Bobruisk. The attacking forces would then roll west in two massive arcs converging on Minsk, the German headquarters, and there surround and destroy the remaining forces of Army Group Center.

Intended to crush the largest force of invaders still holding Russian soil,

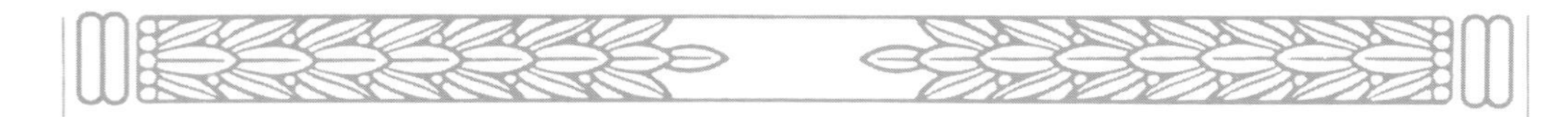

the offensive carried deep historic undertones of Slavic glory and patriotism. Its code name, Operation Bagration, honored General Prince Pyotr Bagration, the Russian hero who gave his life at Borodino defending the motherland against Napoleon more than a century earlier.

In the weeks beforehand, the Russians mustered a force of 166 divisions opposite the German lines, some 1.25 million soldiers in all, not counting administrative staffs and service troops. Supporting the offensive were 2,700 tanks, 1,300 self-propelled guns, 24,000 field guns and heavy mortars, and 2,300 Katyusha rocket launchers. Four air armies deploying 5,300 light bombers and ground attack planes would strike from above.

The Russians outnumbered the Germans by two and a half to one in combat troops, nearly three to one in artillery and mortars, and more than four to one in tanks. Given the Germans' limited supplies of aviation fuel, as well as the fact that Hitler was pulling out planes to send to the West, the Russians won control of the air by default. On the day of the attack, Army Group Center would have scarcely 40 usable fighter planes to fly cover for about 100 bombers.

The offensive began before dawn with a murderous barrage by 10,000 guns and rocket launchers, aimed at key positions along the Third Panzer Army's front. Bombs delivered by a force of more than 1,000 Russian heavy bombers rained down on the fortifications around Vitebsk. Then came the first infantry battalions—not the massive human waves of past Russian assaults, but tightly concentrated spearheads given the mission of gaining tactically important ground along the front of the Third Panzer's IX Corps, northwest of Vitebsk. So selective were these thrusts that for many hours the Germans would regard them as no more than unusually aggressive probes, not a true offensive but a so-called reconnaissance in force.

This was no mere reconnaissance, however. Following the vanguard strike battalions came the infantry divisions, moving in behind a rolling artillery barrage, and after them, the tanks. Overhead, Soviet planes screamed past in wave upon wave, bombing roads and bridges, drilling bunkers and command posts, and strafing troop positions. The IX Corps was struck by 381 sorties during the first day of the battle, and many hundreds more in the days that followed. Air attack had never before been a Soviet strength, and the Germans had not made adequate provision for it. Their field guns, which had been deployed close to the line in open emplacements, took a lethal pounding.

Busch, who on June 22 was at the Berghof hoping for an audience with Hitler, hurried back to his post. No sooner had he arrived than his Third Panzer commander, General Georg-Hans Reinhardt, asked to make a tactical adjustment in the IX Corps line. The answer was worthy of Hitler

Lacking combat experience on the eastern front, Field Marshal Ernst Busch, commander of Army Group Center, readily obeyed Hitler and blindly followed his policy of maintaining a rigid defense. When Busch denied one of his generals permission to fall back, the officer fumed that the "completely inadequate directive from the army group is not a product of purposeful leadership but merely an attempt to carry out orders."

himself—although it lacked the Führer's shrill bark of conviction. No, Busch said: "If we once begin pulling back, we shall simply start floundering about."

But the Third Panzer Army—a panzer army without panzers, like so many shrunken, wasted German units in this third year of fighting on the eastern front—was already floundering. By late afternoon of June 23, the IX Corps, under heavy attack by General Ivan Bagramyan's First Baltic Front, had been pushed back fifty miles to the Dvina River. In the VI Corps sector on the right, where the Third Belorussian Front of General Ivan Chernyakhovsky was attacking along the avenue of high ground between the Dvina and the Dnieper, the German line sagged badly. The hard-pressed garrison at Vitebsk was virtually surrounded. Only a slim, twelve-mile-long corridor linked the city with the German force to the west.

The situation in Busch's center was hardly more encouraging. Soviet guns had opened up against the Dnieper bridgehead of General Kurt von Tippelskirch's Fourth Army on the morning of June 23, blasting away for three hours with an intensity that surpassed anyone's experience. Soon, Russian assault waves that were led by tank formations had ripped open a wide gap east of Mogilev, in the sector defended by the XXXIX Panzer Corps. The army's single reserve formation, Panzergrenadier Division Feldherrnhalle, sped east with orders from Busch to plug the hole. When its commander, Major General Friedrich-Karl von Steinkeller, reported to corps headquarters, he met with a grim reception. "Precisely what hole are you supposed to stop?" demanded corps commander General Robert Martinek. "We've got nothing *but* holes here."

During the next day and a half, the Fourth Army's position further deteriorated. Its left flank, which supposedly was anchored on the fortress city of Orsha, was actually fighting its way to the rear. In the center, the XXXIX Panzer Corps's tattered units streamed back along congested roads

still muddy from recent rains, while fending off assaults from Russian tanks and planes. On the night of the 25th, Steinkeller pulled out his men. "I succeeded, more by good luck than good management, in getting my divisions back across the Dnieper at Mogilev," he later recalled.

By then, the third phase of the Russian offensive, against Jordan's Ninth Army at the edge of the Pripet Marshes, was well underway. Because the marshes constituted a natural barrier, Jordan had concentrated his forces on the drier ground farther north, along his left flank, to defend the rail tracks and highways that led to the fortress city of Bobruisk. But it was through the bogs and thickets of the Pripet that the Soviets were achieving their most surprising advances.

Shrouded by early morning mist, three women stand in the ruins of their home near Smolensk, some 200 miles southwest of Moscow. By the summer of 1944, a great deal of western Russia had been pounded into rubble during three years of almost constant struggle between the Soviet and German armies.

Weeks earlier, the commander of the First Belorussian Front, General Konstantin Rokossovsky, had personally inspected his forward positions in order to scout out the main attack routes. His troops would attack the Germans from two directions, one thrust stabbing west from a Soviet bridgehead on the Dnieper, the other reaching up through the marshy ground in the south. In preparation for the attack, nearly 200 passageways for tanks and artillery were secretly built through the Pripet's bogs and timber pockets, and night patrols removed 34,000 German mines. German prisoners, snatched by scouts, yielded valuable intelligence on the Ninth Army's strength and deployment.

The first Russian assault troops began moving out at six o'clock on the morning of June 24, after a two-hour artillery barrage. In the line's northern sector, opposite the Soviet Dnieper bridgehead, the Ninth Army's XXXV Corps held its turf; the advancing Russians became pinned down in unexpectedly mushy terrain along the banks of the Drut, a Dnieper tributary at the edge of the Soviet bridgehead.

The south told a different story. Here, in the sector guarded by the XLI Panzer Corps, lay a 500-yard stretch of swamp that the defenders had considered impenetrable. Yet across it surged the vanguard divisions of the Soviet Sixty-fifth Army, their tanks rolling along newly laid pathways of logs and tree branches, their infantry sloshing ahead with the benefit of snowshoelike footgear made from woven willow fronds. By mid-afternoon, the XLI Panzer had been rooted out of its front-line trenches and was rapidly pulling back in a 12-mile arc.

Besides having been caught off guard, the XLI Panzer Corps was woefully weak in armor, fielding only two infantry divisions and a mechanized division operating the lumbering and largely ineffective Ferdinand tank destroyers. A quick infusion of reserves might have saved it. And the reserves were available: the superbly equipped 20th Panzer Division, stationed behind the Ninth Army's left wing to defend the Berezina River region. But Jordan, still convinced that that was his weakest sector, decided to keep the division there.

One of the 20th's best units was the reinforced 2d Battalion of the 21st Panzer Regiment. The battalion's 100 Panzer IV tanks were posted along the north-south highway leading to Bobruisk. Receiving no orders of any kind, the battalion commander, Major Paul Schulze, moved out on his own initiative. Spotting some Russian tanks crossing the Berezina, Schulze charged forward with three of his companies to stop them. In the midst of this engagement, an entire Soviet tank corps broke through farther north. Schulze left about 20 Panzer IVs to hold the line at the river and sped on with the rest of his detachment to meet the new threat.

Too late, Jordan realized that the greatest threat to his army lay in the south. Now, in attempting to right his mistake, he made another. No sooner had Major Schulze's intrepid panzer companies engaged the enemy tank corps than Jordan issued orders for the 20th Panzer Division to deploy south toward the Pripet River to stiffen the faltering XLI Panzer Corps. By moving his reserves, which were engaged in heated battle, he opened up holes in his line that the Soviets were able to sprint through. The result was chaos all along the line. "While we were traveling from north to south," reported Schulze, "the Russians smashed the strongpoints of our infantry divisions and overran them. All along my move to the southern sector of Ninth Army, I encountered only formations in flight."

When Schulze and the rest of the 20th Panzer arrived at their new stations, the battle line had virtually disintegrated. Scattered units of the XLI Panzer Corps were falling back on every quarter, heading toward Bobruisk. Worst of all were the air strikes. Soviet planes had the sky to themselves, and they flew more than 3,000 sorties between dawn and dusk of that first day, destroying tanks, smashing gun emplacements, and mowing down retreating troops. No longer a cohesive fighting force, the Ninth Army was approaching a state of imminent collapse.

One hundred miles to the north, on Army Group Center's left wing, the Third Panzer Army, too, was hemorrhaging troops and losing ground at an appalling rate. But despite its worsening situation, the Third Panzer was ordered by the Führer to hold fast. The focus of Hitler's stubborn concern was the fortress city of Vitebsk, the intended cornerstone of the army group's left wing. The entire LIII Corps of the Third Panzer Army, commanded by General Friedrich Gollwitzer and now four divisions strong, had been committed by command of the Führer to the city's defense. Thus, more than one-third of General Reinhardt's total fighting strength was locked into a single position. His remaining two corps, the IX and the VI, were moving rapidly to the rear, too weak to resist the double-pronged Soviet onslaught—the First Baltic Front sweeping past on the left, the Third Belorussian Front hammering through on the right.

A German soldier crawls through a trench dug into the swampy soil of the Pripet Marshes in Belorussia. Having assumed that the marshes were impassable, German troops were caught off guard when Russian forces struck from that region.

Vitebsk, which the high command had expected would engage the prolonged attention of perhaps thirty Soviet divisions, was no more effective at stemming the flow than a pebble in a sluiceway. Within a day, the city lay well in the wake of the Russian advance, nearly twenty miles east of the main German positions.

Reinhardt wanted to evacuate Vitebsk, along the narrow corridor that still connected the city to his VI Corps sector, despite the Führer's "hold fast" dictum. On June 24, he telephoned his pullout request to the chief of the general staff, General Kurt Zeitzler. "We simply must stop the rot at

this stage," he explained. "And I can only do so if I get these troops out in a state to fight again. What I'm afraid of here is the usual 'too late.' "

Zeitzler asked him to wait, and scurried off to confer with Hitler. Ten minutes later, the response came back: "The Führer has decided that Vitebsk will be held."

No sooner had the exasperated Reinhardt put down the phone than he was informed that the potential escape corridor from Vitebsk had come under attack. Then toward nightfall, to his astonishment, he learned that Hitler had signaled General Gollwitzer in Vitebsk directly, giving permission for most of the LIII Corps to withdraw. But there was a grim proviso: "One division is to remain in Vitebsk and continue to hold out. The name of the commander will be reported to me." Sadly, Gollwitzer gave the dubious honor to the 206th Infantry Division, under Lieut. General Alfons Hitter. The order equated to a death sentence.

The smoke of battle billowing around them, two soldiers from a German panzer division pause to slake their thirst during the fighting in Belorussia. The man with the canteen is wearing a sleeve badge he had been awarded for destroying an enemy tank single-handedly.

The next morning, Gollwitzer began sending the three other divisions out along the corridor. But as Reinhardt had predicted, the move came too late. The Soviet pincers clamped down tight, isolating the lead units in a pocket west of town. The escape route was severed, and Soviet machine gunners were already advancing through the rubble-strewn suburbs.

For the next two days, the battered divisions huddled in the deathtrap of Vitebsk, while artillery shells crashed amid them and strikes by Soviet

Sturmovik ground attack planes laid waste their bunkers. Two Russian armies—the First Baltic Front's Forty-third, under General A. P. Beloborodov, and the Third Belorussian Front's Thirty-ninth, commanded by General I. I. Lyudnikov—had taken them under siege. Meanwhile, a stream of radio messages arrived from army group headquarters, reconfirming Hitler's directive to the 206th Infantry: "Hold Vitebsk until relieved."

As if that were not enough, on June 25, the Führer decided that for further emphasis, the sacrificial 206th Infantry Division should receive a formal written order to fight to the end, and that a staff officer from Reinhardt's headquarters should parachute in to deliver it. Reinhardt, already infuriated at the waste of human life, refused to squander another man. In a stormy phone call to Busch, he declared: "Field Marshal, please inform the Führer that only one officer in Third Panzer Army can be considered for this jump, and that's the army commander. I am ready to execute his order." At this bold challenge, Hitler backed down—at least a little. The 206th Infantry would be allowed to expire on its own.

At 5:00 a.m. on June 26, Gollwitzer launched another attempt to break out, this time to the southwest. Some 8,000 troops fought a dozen miles through the Russian lines, under constant air attack. Then, their ammunition ran low. The Russians closed in, wiping them out almost to a man.

Another escape attempt was led by Hitter, who, despite the Führer's order, decided that his 206th Infantry had taken enough punishment. That night, his scouts found a hole in the Russian cordon. He led his men through it, hauling the division's wounded on horse-drawn carts and an artillery tractor. Before it had gone ten miles, the division was encircled. Hitter ordered his men to fix bayonets and charge. Most perished. The few who got through found only brief shelter in a patch of woods, where the Russians rounded them up.

By the morning of June 27, it was all over. The Russians stormed into Vitebsk and captured the remaining Germans. Nearly 20,000 bodies lay in the wreckage of the shattered city or in scattered pockets of the surrounding forest. Only a few men of the LIII Corps made it back to German lines to tell the fate of units that no longer existed.

Every other fortress city along the front was by now coming under similar pressure. One hundred thirty miles to the south, Rokossovsky's armies had closed in on Bobruisk from the west and south, smashing the bridges across the Berezina River and severing all road links to the outside. Ten Russian divisions encircled not only the city but also a large German force in wooded country to the east. Most of Jordan's Ninth Army was thus enmeshed in the Soviet net—the remnants of two entire corps, a total of perhaps 70,000 soldiers.

Bobruisk fell on June 29. During the next six days, some 30,000 troops fought their way out of the Soviet ring, led by grenadiers, a few tanks, and ten assault guns of the XLI Panzer and XXXV corps. Forty thousand others died or became prisoners of the Russians.

Of all the formations in Army Group Center, the Fourth Army had managed to hold itself together the longest. Despite the headlong retreat of its center divisions from their trans-Dnieper bridgehead and a tactical pullback on the left in order to maintain contact with the Third Panzer Army, it had successfully fought off the combined assault of two Russian fronts. But now it, too, was in trouble. With the armies on either side disintegrating, both of its flanks were exposed. Then, on June 26, as the first Russian shock troops punched their way across the swift-flowing Dnieper, the Fourth Army's commander, Tippelskirch, in defiance of every "stand fast" dictum from Hitler and Busch, ordered a general withdrawal.

Two fortress cities lay in the Fourth Army sector—Orsha in the north and Mogilev in the south. Even Tippelskirch did not dare break the Führer's sternest commandment and evacuate a fortress city. So, Orsha fell with all its garrison on June 27, even as Tippelskirch was reading a message from Busch ordering him to hold Mogilev. Near midnight the following night, the Fourth Army was informed that Hitler was now willing to permit the evacuation of Mogilev. By then, no word had been heard from that city for twenty-four hours.

The Fourth Army deployed along the Drut River, less than twenty miles to the west of Mogilev, but was soon forced to retreat again. Its troops had only one tenuous escape route. Behind the army, between the Drut and the Berezina, stretched a forty-mile-wide band of swamp and forest traversed in the center by a single roadway. At the far end, spanning the Berezina at its namesake town of Berezino, was one narrow bridge. The army would have to move the bulk of its men and equipment along this road and across the bridge.

Tippelskirch started down the road on the morning of June 28, to set up new headquarters in Berezino. The trip took nine hours, during which Soviet aircraft attacked the bridge more than twenty-five times. Somehow, in spite of the air assault, Tippelskirch managed to bring most of his army across the river. But as so often happened in the brutal twilight of Army Group Center, the move came too late.

On either flank, the Soviet pincers were already reaching beyond Berezino. To the north, in the gap that had opened between the Fourth Army's left wing and the scattered remnants of the Third Panzer Army, units of the Third Belorussian Front were storming Borisov, another Berezina crossing. Sixty miles to the south, the First Belorussian Front was pushing past

Slutsk, herding the flotsam of Jordan's Ninth Army. Within the next week, the jaws would snap shut at Minsk, the Belorussian capital and army group headquarters—the prime objective of Operation Bagration. Most of the Fourth Army, along with surviving units from the Ninth—at least 100,000 soldiers—would be satcheled into a large pocket southeast of the city.

The shock waves from Army Group Center's collapsing front had by now finally penetrated the high command. At last, Hitler comprehended that Belorussia, not Galicia, was Stalin's summer target. His response was to look for scapegoats. He cashiered Jordan, the Ninth Army commander. Busch, who had too willingly followed Hitler's unrealistic orders, also was relieved. The army group's new commander, Field Marshal Walther Model, took charge on June 28. Endowed with boundless energy and a keen tactical mind—not to mention the Führer's high regard—Model promptly set about regrouping his forces. He shifted reinforcements from Army Group North Ukraine, where he still retained command. And he switched to the fast-paced mobile defense that his predecessor had long recommended but had not been permitted to put into effect.

Model's best efforts could not, however, stop the Russian steamroller. On July 3, the Red Army poured into Minsk, now ablaze from the more than 4,000 delayed-action bombs and booby traps left by the retreating German soldiers. Barely pausing to refuel, the Russians continued their westward sweep, striking on toward the cities of Baranovichi and Molodechno, where Model had hoped to set up a temporary defensive line. So rapid was the

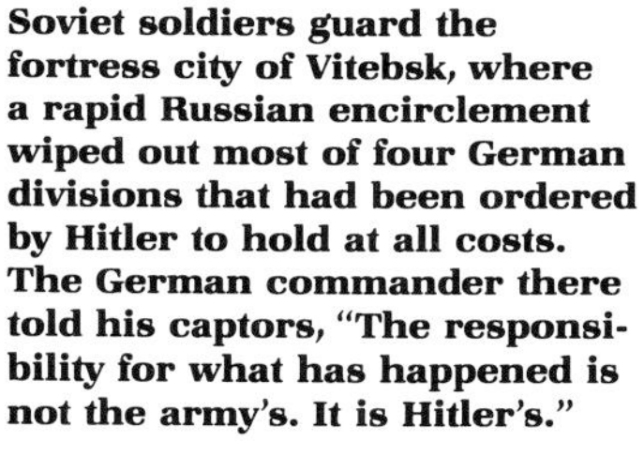

Soviet soldiers guard the fortress city of Vitebsk, where a rapid Russian encirclement wiped out most of four German divisions that had been ordered by Hitler to hold at all costs. The German commander there told his captors, "The responsibility for what has happened is not the army's. It is Hitler's."

Soviet advance that he barely had time to deploy his meager forces. Again, they were driven back.

During the next few weeks, the Germans continued to withdraw their surviving divisions. Reinhardt's Third Panzer Army, now reduced to a single corps, the IX, was pushed back into Lithuania. The Second Army of General Walther Weiss, which had escaped the brunt of the offensive, found itself bracing for a futile defense of Brest-Litovsk, on the old Polish-Soviet border near the Pripet Marshes. The Soviet Second Belorussian Front stayed back to put the squeeze on the 100,000 troops trapped in the pocket behind Minsk. Of those who survived the fighting, the Russians captured 57,000; on July 17, this hungry, tattered throng was marched through the streets of Moscow to illustrate the Red Army's overwhelming victory.

In the twelve savage days of Operation Bagration, the Russians had advanced more than 125 miles and opened a 250-mile-wide breach in the German eastern front. Some 350,000 to 400,000 German soldiers were either killed, wounded, or missing in action. The Russians, according to their own records, had taken 85,000 prisoners, including 21 German generals. Nine other generals had been killed in action or committed suicide. As the high command's war diary noted, the collapse of Army Group Center was a "greater catastrophe than Stalingrad." Indeed, it was the single bloodiest battle of annihilation suffered by the Germans during the entire war.

Some of the Germans who were caught behind the lines were lucky enough—and tough enough—to slip through the Russian net and rejoin their own forces. Moving at night in groups of twenty or thirty—or sometimes fewer, or even alone—they began creeping westward, living off the countryside, a battered ghost army of 10,000 or more. Russian hunting commandos swarmed through the region, and bands of partisans roamed the swamps and forests, all engaged in a massive effort to track them down. In one tactic, German-speaking Soviets wearing captured Wehrmacht uniforms would show up pretending to rally the stragglers, then lead them off to be shot or beaten to death.

No official records serve to document the odyssey of the Wehrmacht refugees; the story has been pieced together from survivors' accounts. Corporal Johannes Diercks, for example, of the 36th Army Artillery Regiment, 20th Panzer Division, found himself alone in a thorn thicket after the German defenses at Bobruisk crumbled, with nothing but his pistol and a map. He was joined by a Corporal Brixius and four other men. Brixius had a compass. That night, they headed northwest.

During the next weeks, the tiny band trekked cross-country, dodging Soviet patrols, gleaning kernels of wheat from fields, raiding an occasional farmstead for milk or bread. Their main diet consisted of blueberries—still

Wagons carry sick and wounded German prisoners of war through Minsk, the capital of Belorussia. In early July, Russian troops crushed German resistance in the area and reoccupied the city of Minsk.

green at the start, but slowly ripening as the weeks went by. During the day, as they hid in the swamps, they could hear the rumble of Soviet divisions moving west past them along the highways, pushing the German lines, and their deliverance, farther away. Other refugees joined them—the crew of a downed Heinkel bomber, a platoon of a *Nebelwerfer* regiment—then went their own way once again.

Diercks had decided to make for East Prussia, the nearest German soil. Heading into what is now Poland, the men stumbled on a Russian field position and were badly shot up. Two of them, seriously wounded, were

Some 57,000 German prisoners who were captured during the Soviet army's campaign in Belorussia are paraded in triumph through Moscow on July 17. Although many onlookers hurled abuse at the captives, some in the crowd pitied them. "Just like our poor boys," murmured an elderly woman.

left to die. Pushing on, the survivors came on a cluster of Soviet mortar and gun emplacements on a hillside just behind the Russian front line. Somewhere ahead stretched the German trenches. Evidently, the men were spotted, for a mortar shell crashed nearby, showering them with splinters of red-hot steel. Each of them took a flesh wound, but none was immobilized. Diercks decided to lie low, and head out again under darkness.

"Shall we manage it tomorrow night?" whispered a soldier named Bauer.

Diercks nodded. "I know one thing for certain; there's no going back."

Just as Diercks and his crew were gathering their last reserves of energy and courage for the final dash to safety, a Soviet sentry spotted them. Diercks whipped out his pistol and shot the man dead. Then, he led his men forward, as a string of enemy mortar blasts erupted from behind them. They ducked into a trench—empty, as luck would have it—then ran on again until they heard the welcome sound of German voices.

Corporal Diercks and his four surviving comrades had left the Berezina on June 27 and had struggled cross-country some 400 miles. The journey had taken them forty-nine days. Of all the 10,000 or more German soldiers who had escaped from the pockets at Minsk and Bobruisk, only 800 are known to have reached their lines.

In mid-July, the thrust of the Soviet summer campaign shifted. With the German forces shoved back in the center to the Vistula River, in Poland,

A Soviet cameraman films *(left to right)* Colonel Paul Beckman, Colonel Wilhelm Alpeter, and Major Reinhardt Moll, officers of the German Ninth Army captured at the town of Bobruisk, 150 miles south of Vitebsk. The prisoners apparently anticipated their capture and donned pressed uniforms and polished boots to meet their conquerors.

Red Army soldiers sweep through the streets of Jelgava, in Latvia, searching for Germans in July 1944. After smashing Army Group Center and retaking Belorussia, the Red Army turned its attention to reclaiming the Baltic States and cutting Army Group North's land route to East Prussia.

Stalin unleashed his armies on both flanks. South of the Pripet Marshes, the First Ukrainian Front's right wing swept past the fortified city of Kovel and on into Poland. The dreaded Galician offensive had finally begun. To the north, the First Baltic Front roared through the gap left by the Third Panzer Army's near-collapse and advanced across Latvia and Lithuania.

Zeitzler, the chief of the general staff, pointed out to Hitler that the First Baltic Front's thrust through Lithuania was about to isolate Army Group North. The group should be quickly withdrawn, Zeitzler argued, in a rare show of backbone. Failing to win Hitler's consent to the retreat, he offered to resign, and when that did not work, he reported himself sick. Hitler responded with a general notice forbidding officers to give up their posts voluntarily. Then, he gave Zeitzler his walking papers. General Heinz Guderian, the champion of blitzkrieg who had participated in the charge on Moscow in 1941 but had been without a command since December of that year, was named the new chief of the general staff.

Like Zeitzler before him, Guderian had no real authority beyond relaying Hitler's orders to the army commanders. For the most part, he confined himself to issuing such inspirational directives as, "We must take the offensive everywhere!" and "The thrust is the best parry!" But on July 23, he did manage to engineer the transfer to Army Group North of General

Schörner. Guderian's hope was that the brutal Schörner would be able to stave off the Russians long enough for Hitler to change his mind and agree to evacuate the Baltic States.

For a while, it seemed that Schörner might succeed. With each new Soviet assault, he gathered his dwindling forces for a counterattack and was able to win back some of the lost ground. He lashed his armies forward with his own special brand of motivational tactics. To one commander, he radioed: "Major General Charles de Beaulieu is to be told that he is to restore his own and his division's honor by a courageous deed, or I will chase him out in disgrace. Furthermore, he is to report by 2100 hours which commanders he has shot or is having shot for cowardice."

By early August, nevertheless, the Russians had encircled Riga and driven a wedge to the sea at the nearby village of Tukums. In a stroke, they had cut the only supply line to Army Group North. The honor of reopening this corridor fell to none other than the remnants of Reinhardt's Third Panzer Army, which the general had managed to preserve in a brilliant withdrawal through Lithuania, and which had now been reinforced with new divisions. On August 17, Reinhardt struck at Tukums with two brigades, supported by the guns of the cruiser *Prinz Eugen* standing offshore in the Gulf of Riga. Three days later, the Germans had reopened the corridor. It was their last victory in the Soviet Union.

During the next four weeks, as the Soviets paused to regroup and resupply, the Wehrmacht divisions trapped in northern Latvia and in Estonia remained in place, fed by the trucks that now ran unimpeded through Tukums and Riga. Then on September 14, through the rising wisps of an autumn fog, the Russians sprang again.

This time, they came on with irresistible violence—twelve armies pushing forward along a 300-mile front, preceded by rolling artillery barrages and backed by massive air support. The Germans reeled back, recovered, and were driven back again. For an entire month, the battle raged with utmost savagery, as Schörner steeled his men to contest every foot of ground. But in mid-October, the First Baltic Front thrust forward once more, driving all the way to the sea. Its left flank now stood poised on the East Prussian border, a boot stride away from German soil.

The destruction of Army Group Center, so much a product of Hitler's dictum against giving up ground, had placed the Reich in immediate peril of losing not merely conquered territory, but the fatherland itself. And farther south, another crisis on the eastern front was unfolding. Hitler's precious Rumanian oil fields—along with his Balkan allies and conquests—were rapidly slipping from his grasp. The Soviet army was now storming through the Balkans with unstoppable momentum. ✚

Yugoslavia in the Grip of Chaos

In April 1941, it took the Germans just a little more than one week to overrun Yugoslavia and not much longer to rip it apart. As bribes to his Axis partners, Hitler awarded chunks of Yugoslavia to Hungary, Bulgaria, and Albania. He claimed the northern part of Slovenia for the Reich, resettling the area with Austrians and subjecting the native population to a ruthless program of Germanization. The Italians seized southern Slovenia and occupied Montenegro and most of Dalmatia. Serbia, the original core of the nation, became a Nazi puppet state under General Milan Nedich. The remaining fragments, the former provinces of Croatia and Bosnia-Hercegovina, were ceded to another new Nazi client, the Independent State of Croatia, under the fascist leader Ante Pavelić, founder of Ustasha, a Croatian ultranationalist terrorist organization.

Yugoslavia was all but wiped off the map. But its tortuous heritage could not be so easily erased. Stitched together after World War I by Pan-Serbian idealists out of the wreckage of the old Habsburg and Ottoman empires, the nation (its name means "Land of the South Slavs") comprised an explosive mixture of ethnically similar peoples with different political, religious, and linquistic traditions. Slovenia and Croatia were Roman Catholic and western in outlook; Serbia, Eastern Orthodox, with an age-old affinity for Russia. Other regions that had been under Turkish rule contained large Muslim populations. And scattered among these groups were a host of non-Slavic minorities.

Hitler's policy of divide and rule provided tinder for these smoldering rivalries. Soon Ustasha was attempting to exterminate the Serbs and other non-Croats living in the new Croatian state. Serbian insurgents fought back, repaying atrocity with atrocity. In regions with mixed populations, a merciless struggle broke out between Catholics, Orthodox, and Muslims. Each community tried to purge its territory of the others and turned to the Axis occupiers for protection. Meanwhile, a Serbian officer named Draza Mihajlović, and Josip Broz, a Croatian Communist known as Tito, raised guerrilla armies to resist the Germans and set the course for the nation's postwar future.

The Germans recast the map of Yugoslavia by giving away pieces of it to its neighbors and by dividing the rest of it into Serbian and Croatian rump states *(left)*. For security purposes, they also split the country into German and Italian zones of interest by drawing a sinuous demarcation line down the middle.

Wearing their distinctive fezzes, ▷ Muslim Yugoslavs of the Waffen-SS Handschar (Scimitar) Mountain Division occupy a jagged peak in northern Bosnia. The Handschar was one of several native units raised by the Germans to fight for the Reich.

Chetnik leaders confer with their commander, Colonel Draza Mihajlović *(second from right).*

Vying for Control

After the capitulation of the Yugoslavian army, a number of Serbian officers and men under the leadership of Colonel Draza Mihajlović took to the mountains to form the first organized resistance against the Axis forces and their Ustasha protégés. Mihajlović and his men constituted the Chetniks, a Serbian monarchist group that took its name from the Serbian guerrillas who had fought against the Turks. Like their predecessors, they wore sheepskin hats adorned with a skull and crossbones, and many of them refused to shave, in accordance with the Orthodox custom of mourning. As the Chetniks saw it, they were mourning their nation's loss of independence.

In late June 1941, following Germany's invasion of Russia, the Chetniks were joined in the field by Tito and his Communists. Tito called his followers Partisans, after the old guerrilla forces that had risen up in Spain and Russia against Napoleon.

Although the Chetniks were recognized by the exiled government and the Allies as the legitimate home army, in the battle for political supremacy, the Partisans enjoyed a huge advantage. Whereas Tito appealed to Yugoslavs of all nationalities, Mihajlović represented only Serbian interests.

Tito relaxes with his dog, Lux. The Alsatian saved Tito's life in 1943 by absorbing a bomb blast intended for the Partisan leader.

German soldiers retrieve the body of a comrade. The cruel nature of the fighting in Yugoslavia prompted many to request duty elsewhere: During a period of several weeks in 1943, more than 1,000 troops volunteered to serve on the eastern front.

Troops of the Waffen-SS Prinz Eugen Mountain Division, recruited from ethnic Germans in Yugoslavia, Rumania, and Hungary, track Partisans in Yugoslavia's Karst region.

The Tactics of Reprisal

During the summer of 1941, the Chetniks and the Partisans briefly suppressed their political differences and joined forces against the common enemy, the Germans.

In turn, the Germans responded with savage reprisals, hoping to terrorize the population into submission. After Hitler signed an order to execute 100 hostages for every German killed, and 50 for every German wounded, Mihajlović ordered the Chetniks to lie low in the Serbian countryside. Besides being deeply suspicious of Tito, he was convinced that continued resistance without significant Allied aid would only lead to a bloodbath that would compromise Serbia's position in the postwar world.

Tito felt no such restraints. He was fighting a classic "people's war of liberation," and he vowed to continue it until the last enemy soldier had been driven from Yugoslavian soil. The Partisans, now fighting Chetniks as well, were left as the only major organized opposition to the Axis forces in Yugoslavia.

A German searches suspected Partisans for weapons. In one retaliatory action in October 1941, the Germans massacred the entire male population of the Serbian town of Kragujevac, shooting 7,000 men and boys.

The Partisans' Narrow Escape

By early 1943, the Partisans had grown powerful enough to seize western Bosnia from Ustasha and threaten German lines of communication to southern Europe. Concerned now about possible Allied landings in the Balkans, the Germans set out to annihilate Tito's threat by launching Operation Weiss, a large-scale offensive to be carried out in the mountainous region northwest of Sarajevo.

Helped by units of Ustashi and Chetniks, the Germans and Italians destroyed 40 percent of Tito's force. But most escaped, marching 100 miles to safety in the forbidding mountains of Montenegro. In a cruel twist, the Germans then turned on the Chetniks, their former allies.

Partisans retreat through a forest near Miljevina in June 1943. The woman on horseback was one of 100,000 women to serve with Tito during the war.

Local peasants help Partisans free an antitank gun from the mud during fighting in western Bosnia in the autumn of 1943.

Tito Emerges on Top

The ability of the Partisans to survive Operation Weiss, coupled with the surrender of Italy in September 1943, marked a turning point in Yugoslavia. Although hard times still lay ahead, Tito had prevailed in his struggle for supremacy over Mihajlović. At the Tehran Conference that November, Churchill, Stalin, and Roosevelt recognized Tito's power by agreeing to channel all future aid to Yugoslavia through the Partisans, thus eliminating the Chetniks as a factor in the war.

Tito's army now numbered some 300,000 men and women—roughly equal to the Axis occupation troops. His forces continued to take control of an ever-increasing proportion of the country until the arrival of the Red Army forced a German withdrawal in March 1945.

Mihajlović, who continued to rescue downed Allied airmen, could never bring himself to believe that Britain and the United States had abandoned him in favor of a Communist. In July 1946, Tito had him executed by firing squad. In death, the Serbian leader joined 1.4 million compatriots who also lost their lives in the years of turmoil—nearly 10 percent of Yugoslavia's prewar population.

Partisans march captured German prisoners through a newly liberated town in October 1944.

СКИ ДЪРЖАВНИ
АВИ ЛСТВО

FOUR

Crisis in the Balkans

When, on July 24, 1944, General Johannes Friessner reported to Wolfsschanze, Hitler's headquarters in East Prussia, he encountered a scene that must have struck him as aptly symbolic. Here in the war room was dramatic evidence of the decline of the Third Reich. The Führer's right arm hung limply in a sling, and both his ears were stuffed with cotton to protect the damaged eardrums. General Alfred Jodl, chief of the operations staff of the armed forces high command, wore a bandage on his wounded head. And the new chief of the army general staff, General Heinz Guderian, was actually a stand-in for Hitler's first choice, General Walter Bühle, who was too severely injured to take the post.

All of this damage was the result of the assassination attempt on Hitler that had taken place four days earlier. A time bomb left by an army conspirator had rocked a building in the compound, injuring Hitler and eighteen others—four fatally—and destroying the Führer's last shred of faith in his generals. "It had already been difficult enough dealing with him," General Guderian wrote after the war. "It now became a torture that grew steadily worse from month to month. He frequently lost all self-control, and his language grew increasingly violent."

In Sofia, Bulgaria, Soviet soldiers and Bulgarian sympathizers rip the Nazi eagle from the German embassy. On September 9, 1944, Sofia became the second of the five Balkan capitals to be wrested from German control that year.

General Friessner had been summoned to receive a new assignment, his second in less than a month. Just three weeks earlier, the stocky fifty-two-year-old infantryman with snow-white hair but youthful face had taken command of Army Group North with characteristic energy and enthusiasm. But like his predecessor, General Georg Lindemann, he soon was sending realistic—and hence pessimistic—reports to Hitler, requesting permission to give up ground and pleading for reinforcements. Hitler quickly decided to reassign Friessner. As a consolation, he would be promoted and swap jobs with General Ferdinand Schörner, a Führer favorite who commanded Army Group South Ukraine.

This army group was deployed along the Rumanian border, a vital but quiet sector of the eastern front. It guarded a region of great importance to the Reich, the Balkan Peninsula, which Hitler described as his "major worry" in the East. The Balkans comprised two German allies, Rumania and Bulgaria, and three nations the Führer had seen fit to occupy early in the war—Albania, Yugoslavia, and Greece. Hitler valued the Balkans for crucial raw materials, such as oil, manganese, and copper, and for their strategic geography. The Balkans had provided a safe southern flank for the invasion of the Soviet Union and a bulwark against an Allied invasion from the eastern Mediterranean. This region, in turn, abutted Hungary, a German ally essential for oil and for its location as a gateway to Austria and the greater German Reich.

The Balkans were considered so important, in fact, that in the spring of 1944, the Germans had assumed the Red Army would strike there next. But the enemy had attacked Belorussia instead, and the southern front had been calm since April. In entrusting Friessner with the new assignment, Hitler assured him: "At this time, there is no danger of a Russian offensive against Army Group South Ukraine. The Russians have expended all their strength against Army Group Center."

Friessner's new front, "where ostensibly nothing was going on," as he wrote later, protected one of Germany's staunchest allies—Rumania. This nation of 20 million people had joined the Tripartite Pact in November 1940, ready "to fight sword in hand beside the Axis powers for the victory of civilization," according to the country's dictator, General Ion Antonescu. A year and a half later, Rumania contributed fourteen divisions to the invasion of the Soviet Union, and these forces helped conquer the Crimea. In addition, the Rumanians provided the Germans with wheat and more than two billion barrels of petroleum a year.

Although substantial strains of fascism infected Rumanian politics, the enthusiasm for the Third Reich had less to do with ideology than with territorial greed. By supporting Hitler's drive eastward, the Rumanians hoped to regain permanently the northeastern lands of Bessarabia and northern Bukovina that had been gobbled up by the Soviet Union before the war. They also wanted to prevail upon Hitler to give back their lost region to the northwest: the northern part of Transylvania, a long-disputed territory that had been ceded to Hungary by German mediators under the so-called Vienna Award of 1940.

Rumania's principal links to the Reich were forged through the person of Ion Antonescu. Nominally subordinate to King Michael, the veteran sixty-two-year-old soldier-statesman ruled as the self-styled "conducator," a title he considered equivalent to that of the Führer and the Italian duce, Benito Mussolini. Like Mussolini, he reveled in self-glorification. In 1941, he

General Johannes Friessner, commander in chief of Army Group South Ukraine *(center)*, discusses the tactical situation in the Balkans with General Otto Wöhler, the Eighth Army commander *(right)*, and Second Panzer Army chief of staff, Major General Helmuth von Grolmann.

annexed the southwestern Ukraine as a new Rumanian province dubbed Transnistria and proclaimed that, henceforth, its major city of Odessa should be called Antonescu, after himself. His shrewdness and soldierly bearing, together with strong doses of anti-Semitism and contempt for the Slavs, won Hitler's trust and confidence. Hitler respected Antonescu more than any chief of Germany's satellites, and he honored him with various medals, including the prestigious Knight's Cross of the Iron Cross, a decoration no other foreigner had yet been granted.

But the turn of the tide on the eastern front during 1943 had taken a toll on Rumanian-German relations. Discontent grew as some 80,000 Rumanian soldiers died during the disastrous battles at Stalingrad and in the Soviet offensive that followed. Allied bombing strikes against the Ploesti oil fields cut petroleum production in half, and the retreat of so many German troops onto Rumanian soil during the spring of 1944 strained the economy. Leading officials began to look for a way out of the war. That spring, several factions undertook secret negotiations with the Allies in Cairo and Stockholm. Even the indomitable Antonescu sent out peace feelers. By the time Friessner took over his new command in the last week of July, the failed attempt on Hitler's life had further shaken Rumanian officials, leaving them "very disillusioned by the war effort," Friessner wrote later.

In addition to finding shaky political conditions, Friessner discovered that the situation at the front was in "sad shape." His command was so short of supplies, tanks, and experienced fighting men that the staff already had drafted a report recommending that the army group be authorized to pull back if faced by a full-fledged Soviet attack. Most shocking to Friessner was a matter the Führer had neglected to mention: Nearly one-third of Army Group South Ukraine's strength was being siphoned off to reinforce Army Group Center. Ten divisions had been transferred since June 30, and an additional division would be taken away during the second week in August. At least six of them were desperately needed panzer divisions.

Friessner did not lack numbers. He had a total strength of forty-seven divisions with more than 800,000 troops, of whom about 360,000 were German. But these units had to cover a front that extended for nearly 400 miles, beginning in the northwest near the Sereth River at the eastern edge of the Carpathian Mountains and running southeastward through Moldavia and Bessarabia to the Black Sea below Odessa. Friessner's left, reaching from the Sereth to the Prut River near the city of Jassy, was covered by Group Wöhler, consisting of the German Eighth Army and the Rumanian Fourth Army. On his right, running from the Prut eastward to the Dniester River and turning southward along its lower reaches, was Group Dumitrescu, with the German Sixth Army and the Rumanian Third Army.

Friessner discovered deficiencies at every turn. In his three armored divisions, he had only 120 tanks fit for battle. His German infantry divisions had plenty of horses but were woefully short of motor vehicles. These units approached full strength in manpower only because they were made up mostly of recently arrived replacements, many of them overage or ill-trained. And the Hungarian and Rumanian railway systems were so inefficient that reinforcements found it faster to march to the front. Supply trains required two to three weeks to make the trip from Germany. Indeed, trains sometimes became so lost that the Luftwaffe had to carry out aerial reconnaissance over hundreds of miles of track in order to locate them.

Worse yet, the command organization resembled a maze. The commander of the German occupation troops, General Erik Hansen, operated independently of Friessner's army group, reporting to the armed forces

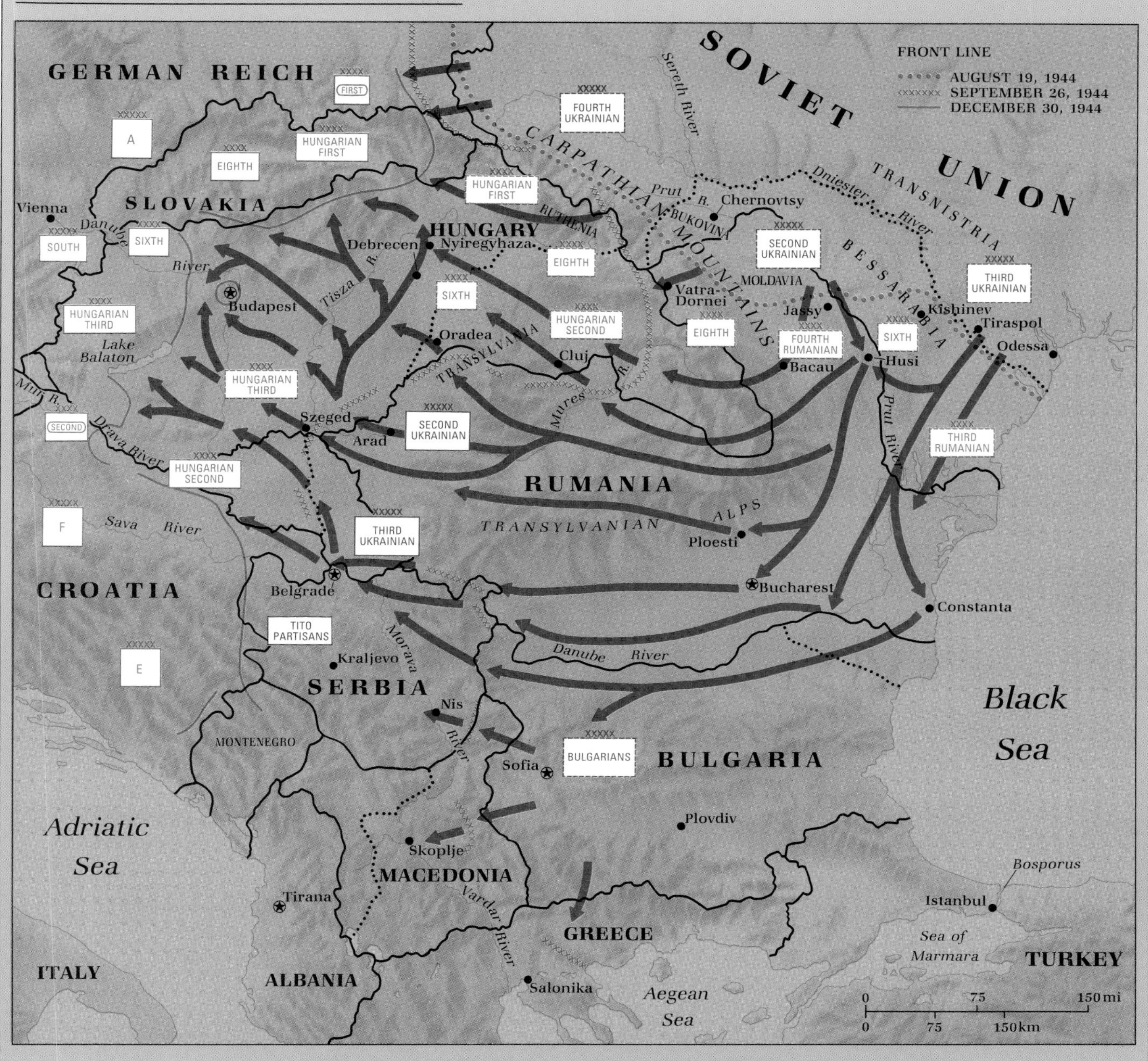

On August 21, 1944, the Soviet Second and Third Ukrainian fronts began a sweep into the Balkans against the combined force of 900,000 Germans and Rumanians of Army Group South Ukraine under General Johannes Friessner. Within three days, Friessner's front line, manned by troops of the Sixth and Eighth armies, was torn open, and the Soviets, now assisted by the defection of Rumania's government, marched into Bucharest on August 31, 1944. By the beginning of October, Third Ukrainian Front troops and Yugoslav Partisans were closing in on Belgrade, having forced back German Army Group F. Farther north, meanwhile, troops of the Second Ukrainian Front penetrated into Hungary. In December, the two Soviet fronts joined up to encircle Budapest, and Friessner, unable to halt the Soviet advance, was dismissed by Hitler.

high command. The chief of Luftwaffe forces in Rumania, Lieut. General Alfred Gerstenberg, who oversaw antiaircraft formations as well as air forces, reported to both the German embassy in Bucharest and to Reich Marshal Hermann Göring. Friessner himself reported to Hitler, directly or through Guderian and the army general staff. To further jumble matters, Antonescu insisted on equality of command; this meant that a Rumanian general, Petre Dumitrescu, exercised tactical control over the German Sixth Army on the army group's right flank.

Concluding that a "political-military disaster was in the offing," Friessner expressed his qualms to both Hitler and the German authorities in Bucharest—and was rebuffed. In response to Friessner's repeated requests to be given command of all German forces in Rumania, Hitler's chief of the armed forces high command, Field Marshal Wilhelm Keitel, only replied: "Hold the front; I will keep your rear secure." Friessner's reports of unreliability in the ranks of Rumanian officers also fell on deaf ears, as did rumors of an impending coup. He later quoted General Gerstenberg as smugly reassuring him that "in case of unrest, one antiaircraft battery would be capable of handling any coup attempt in Bucharest."

The confidence of these other Germans seemed to be borne out in early August when Antonescu visited Hitler at Wolfsschanze. The Führer went out of his way to placate the conducator with talk of new tanks, guns, and secret weapons. Antonescu, in turn, vowed to "remain at Germany's side." Rumania, he averred, would be the "last country to abandon the Reich."

Antonescu's evident honesty and determination impressed both Hitler and the new army chief of the general staff, Guderian. According to Guderian, when he and Antonescu had a private talk about the assassination attempt, the Rumanian expressed shock and added that the "idea of officers taking part in such a coup d'état is unthinkable to us!"

All the same, as Antonescu took leave of Hitler on August 6, the Führer's thoughts were focused on the possibility of perfidy by the Rumanian strongman's nominal superior, King Michael. Hitler instinctively mistrusted monarchs, and recurring reports pegged Michael and his mother as pro-British and the palace as a center of anti-German intrigue. And there were all those rumors from Friessner about an impending coup. As the procession of cars bearing Antonescu started off toward the airfield, the Führer impulsively stepped forward and yelled out a warning: "Antonescu! Antonescu! Don't go into the king's palace!"

On August 8, two days after Hitler's shouted exhortation, the front that had been silent since spring gave signs of renewed activity. Luftwaffe reconnaissance pilots reported columns of Soviet troops moving toward the front. Ten days later, intelligence officers of Group Wöhler, which held

An Allied bombing attack on the Bucharest rail yards in the summer of 1944 further reduces the Wehrmacht's already decimated transportation system. The rail center at the Rumanian capital was an important juncture for shipping fuel from the nearby Ploesti oil fields.

the German left, judged that the enemy would be ready to attack from the north in another day or two, probably in greatest strength astride the Prut River around the city of Jassy.

An assault in this sector represented Friessner's major concern. The Prut bisected the front and, like most rivers in the region, ran northwest to southeast. A powerful attack down this axis could cut off Friessner's entire right wing, including the German Sixth Army. But if he could pivot the wing back—preferably behind the Sereth River but at least to the west bank of the Prut—it would forestall the danger. Pulling back would also shorten his front and lessen dependence on the Rumanian forces. He and Antonescu had repeatedly proposed such a withdrawal to Hitler without success.

Now, with a major Soviet offensive imminent, Friessner reiterated his plea and was once again frustrated. He then resignedly issued orders for the coming battle, professing his confidence that the German troops would stand "shoulder to shoulder with our tested Rumanian comrades."

Shortly after dawn on Sunday, August 20, the Red Army launched its long-delayed attack on the Rumanian flank. General Rodion Malinovsky's Second Ukrainian Front poured down from the north, hitting the German left; General Fyodor Tolbukhin's Third Ukrainian Front struck from the northeast against the German right. The Soviet forces numbered 929,000 troops, supported by 1,890 tanks and assault guns; they possessed so many artillery pieces that on one ten-mile-wide sector of the assault, Malinovsky could mass no less than 4,000 guns—about one every five yards. In every category, they had a huge numerical edge over the combined German and Rumanian defenders: half again as many soldiers, twice as much artillery, nearly five times as much armor, and nearly three times the aircraft.

The two main thrusts occurred about 125 miles apart: from northwest of Jassy in the west and from a bridgehead across the lower Dniester River just south of Tiraspol in the east. By design, both slammed into positions held by the Rumanians. Although some Rumanian troops stood gallantly alongside the Germans, many others abandoned their positions without firing a shot. Trying to stem the flood of men streaming to the rear, the commander of the Rumanian 11th Division laid about him with his whip, then reported to his German superior with tears in his eyes that his division had simply disappeared. Soviet spearheads penetrated a dozen miles on the first day, knifing in behind German formations before the Germans realized their Rumanian allies had given way.

The situation was even worse than Friessner had anticipated. On his far right, one column of Tolbukhin's Third Ukrainian Front drove south to isolate the crumbling Rumanian Third Army and pin it against the Black Sea. Other of Tolbukhin's columns turned west toward the Prut River town of Husi, a rail terminus fifty miles below Jassy. At the same time, the spearhead of Malinovsky's Second Ukrainian Front, the Sixth Tank Army, poured through the breach and bore down on Husi from the north. Friessner saw a double envelopment in the making, with the intended hookup at Husi trapping the German Sixth Army. It was the very kind of classic maneuver that the German panzers had employed against the Red Army with stunning success earlier in the war.

Friessner conferred with Antonescu on August 21, once again proposing to withdraw his right wing behind the Prut, a pullback Antonescu had earlier favored. But now the Rumanian wavered and insisted that he was personally answerable for every inch of ground. Friessner ordered the withdrawal anyway, and that night, Hitler at last agreed to this modest proposal—after the fact.

The order to withdraw came too late. Any semblance of a defensive front was shattered. By Wednesday, August 23, the Axis formations were fighting as disparate islands. The IV Corps had become isolated from the German Eighth Army, and on Friessner's left, its remnants were trying to establish a line on the west bank of the Sereth River near Bacau. Farther east, on Friessner's right, the Soviet armored forces that had sundered his front were operating more than a score of miles behind the German Sixth Army, which was trying frantically to avoid entrapment. These Red Army columns were converging on Husi and the Prut River crossings. Their linkup, which appeared to be a matter of only a few hours, would complete the encirclement of the IV Corps and Sixth Army in the pocket between the Prut and the Dniester and threaten to destroy as many as twenty German divisions.

During that Wednesday, decisive developments were also unfolding in the political sphere. Faced with reports of impending disaster on the battlefields, Antonescu hurriedly sought an audience with King Michael. The dictator went to the palace with his brother, Michael, the foreign minister. Unknown to the Antonescus, the twenty-two-year-old king was party to a conspiracy that had been in touch with the western Allies and intended to stage a coup three days hence. King Michael decided to act sooner. He ordered the Antonescu brothers arrested and interned in the specially ventilated safe his father had constructed to house the royal stamp collection. King Michael went on the radio that night to proclaim the formation of a new government and announce acceptance of an armistice offered by the Soviet Union.

When Friessner heard the news, he immediately took command of all German troops in Rumania. Then, he telephoned the Führer with details of the day's momentous events and a suggestion to withdraw to a new line farther to the north and west, on the border of Hungarian Transylvania. But

General Ion Antonescu of Rumania, a trusted ally of Hitler, observes the battlefront in the Balkans through a trench periscope, while Rumania's King Michael *(center, rear)* stands by. Rumanian armies fought side by side with German troops on the eastern front until August of 1944, when the Soviets overran the country.

Hitler would hear none of it. Outraged by the effrontery of the Rumanian conspirators, he ordered a countercoup, demanding that the king be arrested and the government turned over to Antonescu or, if Antonescu were "no longer available," to some other pro-German general. To achieve his goal, Hitler seized upon the suggestion of General Gerstenberg, the Luftwaffe chief who liked to brag about the capabilities of his antiaircraft gunners, and ordered the 5th Flak Division at Ploesti to capture Bucharest.

Friessner was dubious, and with good reason. As it turned out, he could not find a Rumanian general willing to take over the government even in the unlikely event the Germans could get it back. At half past seven the next morning, 6,000 Luftwaffe flak troops began the thirty-five-mile march to the capital from Ploesti. They captured the radio station but soon ran into stiff resistance from the Rumanian defenders and failed to advance beyond the outlying suburbs. That afternoon, 150 Stuka dive bombers of the German

Fourth Air Force attacked the palace and government buildings in Bucharest. It was another ill-considered scheme that the Führer had seized upon without consulting his commander in the field, Friessner. The bombs united the Rumanian people and provided the government with the pretext for declaring war on the Reich the next day.

The defection of Rumania left Friessner with a desperately fragmented army group. Much of it was threatened with extinction, and Friessner had to give up all hope of extricating his trapped forces—the Sixth Army and the IV Corps of the Eighth Army. While the Stukas were bombing Bucharest on August 24, the Soviet armored pincers had met near Husi on the west bank of the Prut, completing the encirclement of eighteen German divisions in a thirty-mile-wide pocket east of the river. Radio contact with the trapped units was lost, and to monitor events, Friessner had to rely on intercepts of Soviet radio signals.

Inside the pocket, the encircled Germans fought fiercely. Subsisting on corn from the fields, exhausted by the sweltering heat, pounded relentlessly by air and ground fire, they flung themselves desperately against the tightening Soviet grip. Communications had so disintegrated that a Red Army representative trying to negotiate a surrender could find no German authority to negotiate with.

At last, on August 26, the Germans pried open a chink in the Russian armor along the Prut. Elements of two corps, including the 13th Panzer Division, managed to cross the river and take up positions in the woods near Husi. These troops, perhaps 70,000 in all, fought stubbornly, but they, too, were soon outflanked by the Soviet tanks moving swiftly to the southwest. Large pockets of Germans were now trapped on both sides of the river. A number of them managed to escape in small groups and make their way north and west to their retreating comrades.

By August 29, however, the bulk of the troops in both pockets had been killed or captured. Eighteen divisions were swallowed up in the twin encirclements; one division, the 79th, was so decimated that only a single survivor made it to safety in Hungary. These entrapments were even more stunning than the envelopment and destruction of the original Sixth Army at Stalingrad. That storied battle had taken two and a half months; this one required no more than nine days.

Friessner rallied the scattered remnants of his army group and headed toward the mountains bordering Hungary's eastward extension into Transylvania, hoping to establish a new front in the passes of the eastern Carpathians and the Transylvanian Alps. Only four divisions had emerged relatively unscathed from the Rumanian fiasco; they were joined in the columns winding their way up the clogged, single-track mountain road-

Cheered on by Rumanian villagers, a column of Soviet Don Cossacks rides in pursuit of withdrawing German troops. The remnants of Johannes Friessner's Sixth Army fled through difficult mountainous terrain, while most Rumanians celebrated the expulsion of the Nazis.

ways by Luftwaffe flak units, administrative staff, nurses, and other German refugees. "There was no more talk about an organized retreat," Friessner wrote of these last catastrophic days of August. He left behind at least half of his army group, some 180,000 men dead or captured, including 2 corps commanders, 12 division commanders, and 13 other generals.

While Red Army columns pursued the retreating Germans, other Soviet units fanned out to the southwest. The Russians took Ploesti on August 30, capturing the nearby oil fields and airfields, on whose runways sat the last of the Fourth Air Force's bombers and fighters, grounded by lack of fuel. The next day, the Red Army rolled into Bucharest—the first of the capitals of eastern Europe to be "liberated" for the installation of a Soviet-dictated, Communist government. By then, no substantial German unit remained on Rumanian soil, and four more nations lay in the path of the Red Army's multiple spearheads: Bulgaria and Greece to the south, Yugoslavia to the west, and Hungary to the northwest.

The rapid transformation of the war in Rumania influenced events farther afield. Finland, which had long despaired of victory in its tenuous alliance with the Reich, was so encouraged by the coup in Bucharest that the government asked the Soviet Union for peace terms. An armistice was quickly concluded, freeing more divisions of the Red Army for its drive through the Baltic States.

The impact of Rumania was even more dramatic on its southern neighbor, Bulgaria. This little nation of 5.5 million people had enjoyed an unusual relationship with the Reich. Aligning in March 1941, the Bulgarians had provided the Germans with a base for invading Yugoslavia and Greece. They had gone on to supply raw materials, especially grain, and the use of Black Sea ports, as well as to garrison troops for duties in occupied Yugoslavia. But while the Bulgarians declared war on Britain and the United States, old ties of language and culture prevented them from joining the Nazi crusade against the Soviet Union.

As a result, Bulgaria prospered. The country received high prices for its food exports, and annexed ancestral lands from Yugoslavia and Greece. "To be sure," a Bulgarian politician recalled later of his country's new geopolitical strength, "we had somewhat of a bad conscience because we had not fought for and conquered but rather received it as a gift."

By the time the Red Army invaded Rumania, however, Heinz Guderian was getting disquieting reports from the German army's military mission in Sofia, the Bulgarian capital. The premature death of King Boris in 1943—probably from a heart attack but widely attributed to German malevolence—had stirred local discontent. And now that the tide of war had

sharply turned in favor of the Russians, officers in the Bulgarian army were openly questioning the partnership with Germany. Guderian asked Hitler to put a stop to shipments of armor to Bulgaria and to withdraw what had already been sent. The Führer refused, insisting the Bulgarians so detested bolshevism that they would never abandon Germany.

But on August 26, three days after the Rumanian coup, the Bulgarian government gave every sign it wanted to do just that. Hoping to stave off the Red Army threatening its border fifty miles north of Sofia, the Bulgarian government reaffirmed its neutrality, asked the United States and Britain for peace, ordered all German troops to go home, and promised to disarm any Germans crossing over into its territory from Rumania.

This was sufficient to infuriate the Führer, who ordered Germans in Bulgaria to resist, but not enough to satisfy the Soviets. Stalin dispatched his top military tactician, General Georgy Zhukov, to Rumania to coordinate an invasion of Bulgaria. On September 5, alleging that a neutral Bulgaria could serve as a refuge for the retreating Germans, the Soviets declared war. Zhukov massed three rifle armies and a mechanized corps of Tolbukhin's Third Ukrainian Front on the border between the lower Danube River and the Black Sea. At 11:00 a.m. on September 8, elements of the Soviet Fifty-seventh Army invaded Bulgaria. They were greeted by Bulgarian infantry lining both sides of the road to welcome them.

Germans living in Bucharest were caught by surprise as King Michael took control of the government and announced an armistice with the Soviets on August 23, 1944. At left, a group of Nazis who have been arrested by Rumanian soldiers are marched past the city's athenaeum. Below, German civilians who sought sanctuary in the Reich's embassy as the coup unfolded wait outside the legation to be evacuated.

Bulgaria declared war on Germany that night. On the next day, September 9, a coalition known as the Fatherland Front, which included domestic Communist leaders and a leftist officers' organization called *Zveno,* took over the government in a bloodless coup. The Red Army swiftly occupied the country and took command of the 450,000-man Bulgarian army, including the eighty-eight Panzer IVs and fifty self-propelled assault guns that Guderian had vainly tried to get back a few weeks earlier. Bulgarian soldiers would soon see combat for the first time in the war in

next-door Yugoslavia against their former German allies, whom they had helped with occupation duties in that splintered nation.

In Yugoslavia, the Red Army and its new Bulgarian partners would encounter German defenders from a completely separate command. Friessner and his Army Group South Ukraine had retreated to the Hungarian frontier. The Germans in Yugoslavia belonged to the Southeast Theater, with headquarters in the capital, Belgrade, under Field Marshal Maximilian von Weichs. Weichs was a sixty-three-year-old veteran of various commands that ran the gamut of the war, from France to the Soviet Union. He now led two different units, Army Group E, occupying the Greek mainland and the Aegean Islands, and Army Group F in Yugoslavia and Albania. Together, the two army groups comprised some thirty divisions of about 500,000 soldiers. Although Weichs and Friessner were now engaged in a common effort, the defense of the southern flank against the Soviet onslaught, they reported through separate channels—Weichs via the armed forces high command, Friessner via the army high command. And Hitler's hypersensitive security regulations prevented them from communicating with each other to coordinate their actions.

Throughout the war, these Southeast Theater troops had been charged with a dual mission. One was the military task of defending the coasts of the Balkan Peninsula against an Allied invasion and protecting lines of communication along the Reich's southern flank. The more difficult mission was subduing the guerrilla movements that arose in all three countries. Internal resistance was particularly fierce in Yugoslavia, a cauldron of discordant peoples whose hatred had been brought to a boil by the harsh occupation. After conquering Yugoslavia in April 1941, the Germans had presided over a cruel dismemberment of this already-divided land of 14 million people. They gave segments of its land to Italy, Bulgaria, Albania, and Hungary and partitioned the rest into spheres of influence. Two large rump states, Croatia and Serbia, remained under puppet governments.

Soon after the invasion, two guerrilla movements with opposing goals emerged. One, the royalist Chetniks under Colonel Draza Mihajlović, fought against the German occupiers to restore the monarchy. The other, the leftist Partisans under Josip Broz—the Marxist revolutionary known as Tito—wanted to install a Communist regime. The Chetniks and Partisans waged hit-and-run raids with such cunning that they tied down at least a dozen Axis divisions throughout most of the war.

But the two guerrilla forces fought each other with even greater guile and ferocity. The Partisans, with their superior political skills in organizing the peasantry at home and in cultivating aid from abroad, gradually took over the rebellion. Surprisingly, weapons and other support came not only from

On August 31, 1944, soldiers of General Rodion Malinovsky's Second Ukrainian Front are welcomed as they enter Bucharest. During the previous week, the Rumanian capital had been the target of Luftwaffe bombing—a belated and vain German effort to recapture the city.

the Partisans' ideological ally, the Soviet Union, but also from the United States and Britain, who abandoned Mihajlović's forces as the weaker of the two movements and the one tainted by collaboration with the Germans.

Thus, in September 1944, after Rumania defected and Bulgaria caved in, the German defenders confronted a double threat. Tito's Partisans had now grown into a well-equipped force of 300,000 irregulars. They were ready to link up with the Soviet and Bulgarian forces massing on the borders of Bulgaria and Rumania. From Belgrade, the Southeast Theater commander, Field Marshal Weichs, wrung permission from Hitler to issue a series of orders for Army Group E to begin the evacuation of Greece. The mission of guarding against an Allied landing there had been rendered irrelevant by the invasions of France that summer. Now, the need to get out was urgent. Weichs needed help in defending Yugoslavia. Moreover, the new

Soviet presence in Bulgaria and the Bulgarian-occupied Macedonian region of northern Greece threatened to cut off Army Group E's line of retreat.

The pullback proceeded at an agonizing pace. The full evacuation of Rhodes, Crete, and the other Greek islands was not authorized by Hitler until September 15, and it was further slowed by a lack of air transport. Weichs unaccountably waited until October 3 to order complete withdrawal from Greece and Albania, and another week passed before the order was executed. By then, a contingent of British troops had already landed in southern Greece, and bands of Greek guerrillas—as in Yugoslavia, there were opposing resistance groups composed of royalists and leftists—harried the retreating Germans.

Meanwhile, the Soviet invasion of Yugoslavia had already begun. On September 22, advance elements of Tolbukhin's Third Ukrainian Front struck westward across the Danube. They aimed at Belgrade, the capital of the puppet state of Serbia and capital of prewar Yugoslavia. Within a fortnight, eastern Serbia swarmed with enemies of the Reich. From the Third Ukrainian Front in Bulgaria and southern Rumania came nineteen rifle divisions and more than 500 tanks. Farther north, the left wing of Malinovsky's Second Ukrainian Front swept through upper Serbia en route to Hungary. To the south, three Bulgarian armies—supported by Stuka dive bombers, much to the consternation of their former German allies—advanced against the Serbian city of Nis, 125 miles southeast of Belgrade. And Tito's Partisans, fortified with the initial shipments of some 100,000 rifles, 68,000 machine guns, and other weapons that would arrive from the Soviet Union during the following weeks, already had hooked up with Red Army spearheads below Belgrade.

Army Group F was doomed from the start. Badly outnumbered, the troops were largely overage soldiers, equipped with few tanks and little motorized transport. And Weichs committed them piecemeal. Against all these odds, they fought with tenacity. On the roads to Belgrade, German commanders pulled together what organized infantry, tanks, and assault guns they could. These defensive units allowed Soviet tanks to rumble into point-blank range, then blasted them until the defenders themselves were swept away by overwhelming forces. German reinforcements hurrying north from Greece by train were slowed when Soviet and Bulgarian troops repeatedly cut the rail line. It took one division two full weeks to reach Belgrade, a journey that would normally take only one day.

The first of the Soviet forces' main objectives, the city of Nis, fell on October 15. Four days later, the Partisans entered Belgrade, catching rides on Red Army tanks so they could claim precedence over the Soviets, whom Tito had persuaded to request, retroactively, official Partisan permission to invade Yugoslavia. Bitter fighting for the capital had begun earlier, and often raged house to house. By October 20, the Partisans and their invited liberators had cleared the city and proclaimed victory.

While Army Group F retreated and formed a new line near Srem, 50 miles northwest of Belgrade, their comrades from Army Group E in Greece continued to trickle northward through the southern Yugoslavian province of Macedonia. The last units of these late arrivals crossed the frontier on November 2. Then, near the rail center of Skoplje, 200 miles south of Belgrade, they held off Soviet and Bulgarian divisions long enough to ensure a successful withdrawal to the northwest through Kraljevo. But the frustrations of the tardy withdrawal were illustrated by the wastage of manpower: An estimated 30,000 German troops, as well as 60,000 Italians,

German sappers remove explosives set by partisans along an important military supply line in northern Greece. Local partisans frequently sabotaged German communications in the Balkans, considerably aiding the Soviet war effort and hindering Nazi retreats.

were stranded on Crete and on other Greek islands for lack of air transport.

With most of Serbia secure, the bulk of the Soviet armies left the remainder of the fighting in Yugoslavia to Tito's Partisans and drove north into Hungary. There, they joined the battles that had been raging since the end of August, once again facing Friessner's army group in the climactic campaign against Germany's southern flank.

The Hungary that Friessner and his troops were called upon to defend had been a lukewarm partner at best. Hungarian ties with Nazi Germany had more to do with naked self-interest than with political ideology. This nation of about nine million people had joined the Axis in 1940 out of a dread of Soviet communism, as well as the desire to regain some of the land lost during World War I when it was forced to surrender more than two-thirds of its territory. Lining up with Hitler allowed the Hungarians to take back northern Transylvania from Rumania and the part of eastern Czechoslovakia known as Ruthenia. In return, the Hungarians exported crude oil, manganese, and bauxite to the Reich and initially contributed one corps of troops for the German invasion of the Soviet Union, which they anticipated would lead to a quick victory. When that hope faded in the fall of 1941, the Hungarians recalled all but a token contingent of troops deployed along their own frontier, and relations with Germany cooled.

Early in 1943, Hungary began sending out peace feelers to the West. By March of 1944, Hitler was so concerned about these "treacherous intrigues" that he ordered German troops to occupy the capital of Budapest and other key centers. Occupation authorities then installed a pro-German cabinet and began deporting Hungary's Jews to the gas chambers at Auschwitz.

Hitler allowed Admiral Miklós Horthy de Nagybánya to remain in power as the chief of state, although he loathed the old man. Now in his seventy-seventh year, Horthy had served since 1920. He was a popular leader and a shrewd and often-courageous pragmatist. In July 1944, seven weeks after the Germans had started the deportation of the Jews, Horthy stopped it in order to protect Budapest's prosperous Jewish community of business and professional people, who were essential to the Hungarian economy. On August 29, in the wake of the Rumanian collapse, he replaced the pro-German cabinet and resumed secret approaches to the western Allies.

"Look, my friend," the wily old leader told Guderian when the German army chief visited Budapest at the end of August, "in politics you must always have several irons in the fire." One week later, on September 7, Horthy issued an ultimatum demanding five fresh panzer divisions be sent to his country within twenty-four hours, or he would ask the enemy for an armistice. Guderian called it outright extortion but began scraping together enough armor to mollify Horthy.

Smoke from an Allied bombing attack billows over the steeples and domes of Budapest in the summer of 1944. Occupied by the Nazis in the spring of that year, the Hungarian capital was a target of regular Allied air missions until the Russians seized the city in February 1945.

As General Friessner moved his battered army group into position at the beginning of September, the situation seemed woefully reminiscent of the one that had prevailed a fortnight earlier in Rumania. He trusted neither the loyalty nor the ability of the Hungarian troops. And he was being asked once again to defend too long a line, this time with even fewer resources than those under his command in Rumania.

The new defense line coincided roughly with the mountainous rim of northern Transylvania, the region recovered by Hungary from Rumania in 1940. The eastern Carpathians in the northeast and their southwest extension, the Transylvanian Alps, protruded eastward from the prewar Hungarian frontier into old Rumania like the head of an enormous horse. The point of this bulging salient, known as the Szekler Corner, extended some 225 miles from the old border. It meant that Friessner had to cover a meandering front some 500 miles long with a total of twenty-eight severely depleted German and eighteen very weak Hungarian divisions—less than 200,000 soldiers in all.

Friessner knew this was impossible, even though substantial portions of the Red Army were now turning south to deal with Bulgaria and Yugoslavia. He feared another double envelopment of the kind that had nearly destroyed the Sixth Army in Rumania. He knew that another Soviet force, the

Fourth Ukrainian Front, was deployed farther to the north. Fretting that this force and Malinovsky's Second Ukrainian Front sweeping to the south would outflank him and sever the Szekler salient, Friessner lobbied for permission to pull back to the prewar Hungarian border. Admiral Horthy seemed willing to abandon northern Transylvania, but Hitler refused.

Hitler explained his refusal in a meeting with Friessner on September 10 in East Prussia. The Führer fully realized that Hungary was of prime strategic importance. With Rumania gone, Hungarian wells pumped one-third of Germany's crude oil. But the Führer was convinced that the Red Army would not mount a major offensive against Friessner in Transylvania.

During the fight for Hungary in the autumn of 1944, a German self-propelled antitank gun *(above)* fires a round at an advancing Russian tank near the town of Szekesfehervar about thirty-five miles southwest of Budapest. As the Germans withdrew, they often carried the wounded in handcarts *(right).*

Instead, he said, the Soviet movement into Bulgaria signaled a revival of the old Russian aim to dominate the Balkans and control the Dardanelles. This southward thrust would bring the Russians into conflict with Britain's historical interests, the Führer told Friessner, marking a turning point in the war as these erstwhile allies fought for control of that region. Buoyed by this illusion, Hitler came down to earth long enough to grant Friessner a partial withdrawal in Transylvania to behind the Mures River.

To win this concession, Friessner had to agree to two unrealistic stipulations. One was to bend his new line outward to cover the manganese mines at Vatra-Dornei, some 150 miles east of the prewar Hungarian frontier, even though the miners themselves had already abandoned them. The other stipulation was that Friessner make the Mures his defensive line for the winter. Friessner completed the withdrawal by September 15 and managed to hold his own behind the river for a week or so in rugged mountainous terrain up to 8,000 feet high.

A Coup in the Citadel

When Adolf Hitler learned from secret reports in September of 1944 that his ally, Admiral Miklós Horthy de Nagybánya, the Hungarian head of state, was planning to make a separate peace with the Soviets, he angrily summoned his favorite commando leader, SS Major Otto Skorzeny, and charged him with preventing the capitulation. Stormed the Führer: "You must be prepared to seize the citadel of Budapest by force."

Skorzeny and his special forces infiltrated Budapest, and when Horthy announced the intended armistice with the Russians on October 15, the Germans struck swiftly. They kidnapped Horthy's son Niki and bundled him off to Vienna.

The following morning at six o'clock, Skorzeny and his men entered the Burgberg, the citadel that contained Horthy's palace and other government buildings. Led by a Panther tank that burst through a barricade at Horthy's residence, the Germans took the Hungarian troops by surprise and encountered little resistance. Within thirty minutes, the citadel was occupied and Horthy was in German hands.

The regent was taken to Germany, where he sat out the war as a "guest of the Führer." A pro-Nazi puppet was installed as premier.

Antitank *Panzerfausts* at their sides, German troops stand guard outside the government building where Horthy was arrested.

SS Major Otto Skorzeny *(left)*, accompanied by his chief of staff, Captain Adrian von Fölkersam *(right)* and an aide, crosses a square in the citadel after the coup d'état.

The bodies of two of the four Germans killed in the operation lie near captured weapons.

But the Soviets were regrouping and gathering new strength. They were also shifting their weight westward, along the bottom of the Szekler salient toward the Rumanian city of Arad.

On October 6, the Soviets struck in force from the southwestern corner of Rumania against the vulnerable German right flank. Some sixty-four divisions strong, including twenty-two Rumanian divisions, they drove to the northwest, bursting out of the Transylvanian Alps between Arad and Oradea, scattering the newly formed Hungarian Third Army, and spilling into the lowlands of Hungary proper. Some units penetrated 50 miles in just three days and soon reached the Tisza River at Szeged, scarcely 100 miles southeast of Budapest.

But the key was the armor on the Soviet right, which drove north toward Debrecen, Hungary's third-largest city. The aim, as Friessner had anticipated, was to hook up with advance elements of the Fourth Ukrainian Front, which were driving south from the area where the Czechoslovakian, Polish, and Ukrainian borders met. The Russians intended to pinch off the Szekler salient, trapping the Axis troops in Transylvania.

While Hitler wavered, Friessner acted. On his own, he ordered the forces in the salient—Army Group Wöhler, comprising the German Eighth Army and the Hungarian First and Second Armies—to execute a fighting withdrawal westward to the Tisza River. These troops began pulling back from their mountain strongholds, including the city of Cluj in the Carpathians, a Transylvanian traffic center that the Germans had clung to stubbornly.

At the same time, Friessner moved to block the Soviet attempt to trap these troops before they could withdraw behind the Tisza. He brought back a panzer division that had been deployed in Budapest by Hitler for political reasons and moved up the first of four additional panzer divisions the Führer had committed to Hungary in response to Admiral Horthy's earlier ultimatum. On October 10, racing across flat ground, these phalanxes hit from east and west against the flanks of the Soviet Sixth Guards Tank Army, advancing north toward Debrecen, just inside the old Hungarian border. The surprise strike, reminiscent of blitzkrieg days, temporarily cut off three Soviet corps. For the next four days, tank battles raged across the plains near Debrecen, so fierce and confusing that the rival commanders often could not tell friend from foe. In one day, the 23d Panzer Division alone accounted for the destruction of twenty-six of fifty attacking Soviet tanks.

The Soviet armored forces shook free from these seesaw struggles and on October 20—the same day Belgrade fell 200 miles to the south—seized Debrecen. Two days later, Soviet spearheads captured Nyiregyhaza, a city 35 miles to the north of Debrecen, and pressed on 15 miles to the upper Tisza River. But there was no linkup with the Fourth Ukrainian Front, which

The Margaret Bridge, a strategic span across the Danube in Budapest, lies wrecked after a German demolition team accidentally blew it up on November 4, 1944. Nazi engineers had set explosives on many of the Danube bridges in order to impede a Soviet advance.

had moved eastward into Czechoslovakia. The following day, Friessner, with the line of retreat blocked for his forces still in northernmost Transylvania, relied on his reinforcements from the III Panzer Corps. The fresh German armor slammed into the Soviets from the west while Wöhler's trapped soldiers attacked from the east. The surprise blows converged between Debrecen and Nyiregyhaza; their impact scattered the Soviets, destroyed an estimated 600 Russian tanks, and resulted in the recapture of Nyiregyhaza on October 26. The route was now open for Wöhler's columns to retreat behind the Tisza and form a new defensive line with their colleagues of the rebuilt Sixth Army. Not since the Soviet breakthrough in Rumania had Friessner been able to patch together a continuous front.

In Budapest, meanwhile, the Germans had scored another kind of success intended to ensure that Hungary would remain in the war. Having learned that Admiral Horthy was negotiating for a separate peace with the Soviets, Hitler dispatched a commando team, led by SS Major Otto Skorzeny, to Budapest to prevent the defection of the government. On October 15, four hours before Radio Budapest announced acceptance of the Soviet peace terms, the commandos kidnapped Horthy's son and later stormed the Burgberg, the citadel overlooking the Danube that served as the seat of the Hungarian government. With the Germans in firm control, Horthy agreed to abdicate and appointed a new government headed by Ferenc Szálasi, leader of the pro-Nazi Arrow Cross party.

The twin German victories, on the battlefield and in Budapest, brought only a brief respite for Friessner and his newly renamed Army Group South. (The word *Ukraine* had finally been dropped in light of the nearly 500 miles that now separated the army group from that part of the Soviet Union.) The recent armor engagements had left him with only sixty-seven tanks in four panzer and two panzergrenadier divisions. The Russians now controlled the eastern third of Hungary proper. Friessner also had no secure link with Field Marshal Weichs's Army Group F to the south, which had taken up positions along the lower Tisza in Yugoslavia after the fall of Belgrade.

Morale among the Hungarian troops was so shattered that entire units, together with many high-ranking officers, deserted to the Red Army. Particularly galling was the manner of defection chosen by the army chief of staff, General Janos Voros, who had driven over to the other side in the luxurious Mercedes sedan that his German counterpart, Heinz Guderian, had recently given him. The Germans in Hungary were still, as Hitler had said several weeks earlier, "dancing on a volcano."

The vulnerability of Friessner's new front was demonstrated at the end of October. On the 29th, the Soviet Forty-sixth Army, supported by mech-

To resupply the troops trapped in Budapest during the Soviet siege in January 1945, more than forty-five German gliders aimed for a small landing strip in one of the city's parks. The flight above ended in disaster.

anized units, crossed the lower Tisza River and turned Friessner's southern flank manned by the Hungarian Third Army. The Soviets raced northwestward between the Tisza and the Danube, behind the German front. By November 4, they had driven nearly eighty miles, all the way to the outskirts of Budapest, before the German panzers smashed into their right flank, forcing them to pull back several miles to the southeast.

This Soviet thrust was the beginning of the new phase in the campaign that Friessner labeled the "battle for Budapest." The lovely old city on the Danube was as much a political prize as a military one, and the Soviets renewed their efforts to capture it on November 11. During the succeeding weeks, instead of attacking head-on, they carried out a series of peripheral maneuvers intended to encircle the city. From Yugoslavia, the main forces of Tolbukhin's Third Ukrainian Front, fresh from the liberation of Belgrade, swung north and joined in the hard fighting brought on by these elaborate maneuvers. Friessner had to abandon the Tisza Line and fall back so close to Budapest that, to his disgust, some of his Hungarian officers spent the nights at home in their own beds and commuted to the front on streetcars.

In December, Friessner clashed repeatedly with Guderian, who had been reduced to serving as the Führer's mouthpiece. Facing numerical odds he estimated at ten to one against him, Friessner opposed Hitler's orders for

These somber, battle-weary troops riding atop an armored vehicle were among the few Germans who managed to break out of the Soviet encirclement of Budapest. The Russians overran the city on February 13, 1945.

a house-by-house defense of Budapest on the grounds that the citizens, defiantly preparing for Christmas, were not ready and that they would turn against the Germans when pressed. He also wanted to delay Hitler's demand for a counterattack until the swampy ground had frozen solid. On December 22, Guderian fired Friessner and replaced him with General Otto Wöhler. Four days later, the Soviets succeeded in encircling Budapest.

Hitler vowed to lift the siege of Budapest and to defend the Hungarian oil fields. The capital and its environs—an island of some 188,000 German and Hungarian troops trapped with a population of nearly one million civilians in a sea of Soviets and Rumanians—had become in Hitler's eyes a symbol of the Reich's resolve, much as Stalingrad had once been. The oil fields, which lay behind the new front in western Hungary, near Lake Balaton, pumped out the lifeblood of the Reich's sputtering war machine. In a desperate bid to break through to Budapest, Hitler, without consulting Guderian, ordered the transfer of General Herbert Gille's IV SS Panzer Corps from near Warsaw—just as the Red Army was on the brink of unleashing their long-awaited final offensive through Poland.

Beginning on January 1, 1945, Gille's panzers struck again and again at the ring of armor that the Red Army had forged around Budapest. They drove first from the northwest, then swung around counterclockwise and attacked from the west and south. But in four weeks of trying, the SS troops failed to break through. Meanwhile, the Second Ukrainian Front poured into Pest, the eastern half of the Danube-divided city and—amid what a German war correspondent described as a "nauseating stench of decaying corpses"—captured the last of the defenders there on January 19. Across the river on the fortresslike heights of Buda, the last Germans held out among the ruins for three additional weeks, sustained by a diet of horsemeat soup and bread and Hitler's promises of relief.

By February 12, however, it was clear these promises would not be fulfilled. That night, the eve of the capitulation of Budapest, some 16,000 Germans tried to fight their way out of the encirclement. Only 785 soldiers actually reached German lines; the rest were trapped and shot down within a few miles of the city. By the perhaps exaggerated Soviet count, the battle for Budapest had cost the German and Hungarian armies more than 50,000 dead and 138,000 taken prisoner.

German troops would go on fighting and dying in western Hungary until April, but like the battle for Budapest, it was a tragic sideshow. The main event—the "beginning of the last act," as Guderian termed it—already was being played out to the north. There, even before Budapest fell, the momentum of the massive Soviet offensive in Poland had already carried the Red Army into the Reich itself. ✚

The Uprising in Warsaw

On August 1, 1944, some 25,000 patriots of the underground Polish Home Army, along with thousands of civilians, took to the streets of Warsaw to wrest the city from its German occupiers. Led by General Tadeusz Komorowski, code-named Bor, the Poles were determined to protect the capital from destruction by vengeful Germans retreating from the eastern front and to reassert Polish independence before the advancing Soviets arrived in force. Although the rebels realized that their revolt would succeed only with Allied help, they wished to prevent at all costs a Soviet-controlled government in Warsaw.

Heartened by the sound of the Red Army's artillery and encouraged to fight by a Soviet radio appeal, Poles of all ages and political persuasions attacked German positions in and around Warsaw.

When SS chief Heinrich Himmler got word of the uprising, he flew from his headquarters in East Prussia to Poznan, roughly 160 miles west of Warsaw, to organize the German response. To reinforce the troops stationed in Warsaw, he gathered the forces available in the vicinity, including a police detachment and two unruly SS units, one made up of ex-convicts and former

Soviet prisoners of war, the other of Ukrainian collaborationists who nursed a hatred of Poles and Communists. His orders for these 12,000 men read in part: "Every inhabitant of Warsaw must be killed. Warsaw must be razed to the ground, and thus a frightening example for the whole of Europe will be created."

Polish partisans attack a German-held building in Warsaw. The

rebels left a mark that meant "Poland Fighting" *(above, left).*

A Polish partisan rips a Nazi flag from a building. When the rebellion erupted, Varsovians destroyed Nazi symbols and raised the flag of Poland.

From his hideout, a Home Army sniper waits for a target *(above)*. To conserve ammunition, Polish fighters let the enemy get as close as possible before firing.

A Stunning Blow by the Home Army

Despite warnings from German intelligence that trouble was brewing, the Germans stationed in Warsaw were stunned by the ferocity of the Home Army's initial assault. By August 3, the insurgents controlled three-quarters of the capital. With barely enough food and ammunition to last a week, they struck at German supply depots and ammunition dumps as well as administrative offices. The Germans lashed back from strongholds fortified with concrete and ringed by barbed wire. At the Vistula River, the eastern boundary of Warsaw proper, the partisans tried to seize key bridges, but were quickly repelled.

On August 4, Himmler's hastily assembled force, supported by tanks, heavy artillery, and bombers, slammed into Warsaw from the west and embarked on a bloody killing spree that left thousands of civilians dead in just a few days. Most of the Home Army was driven into Old Town, the city's medieval section, where they fought with obsolete firearms, homemade grenades, and when ammunition ran low, paving bricks. The fighting surged back and forth until mid-August, when the German Ninth Army was brought in for a more disciplined attack against the rebels.

◁ **A group of partisans seizes a German staff car. Captured vehicles helped speed communications among the scattered forces of the Home Army.**

Smoke pours from the telephone exchange in Warsaw. After driving out Germans by torching the building, the rebels moved in and quickly doused the flames.

Germans prepare Goliaths, self-propelled vehicles with explosive charges detonated by remote control.

A Vicious German Response

Troops of the German Ninth Army attacked with tanks, rocket launchers, and mortar fire from field artillery and gunboats on the Vistula. Warplanes bombed with impunity. The ferocious assault ignited fires within Warsaw and soon turned it into a furnace. One shaken partisan wrote, "Every hour, enemy Stukas fly over from the airfield, dropping bombs on the city. It is outright slaughter; we do not have one antiaircraft gun in the entire city."

German soldiers on a Warsaw street load rockets onto a launching frame.

Assault guns sit deserted in downtown Warsaw. The unwieldy vehicles were easy prey for rebels armed with Molotov cocktails.

The Prudential skyscraper, a Warsaw landmark that had been transformed into a Home Army stronghold, crumbles during a

Germans blindfold Countess Tarnowska and a Home Army delegate before talks.

German bombardment.

Waiting in Vain for the Russians

Time and time again, Polish insurgents in Warsaw tried to break through the German ring and relieve their Home Army compatriots trapped in the Old Town district. Finally, near the end of August, many of the Old Town fighters escaped through the sewers, some fleeing north to the suburb of Zoliborz while others scrambled south to the district called Center City. Left behind were 2,500 wounded partisans. By now, 30,000 civilians lay dead, and more than 50,000 had been wounded. With supplies quickly dwindling and the Ger mans tightening their grip on th city, the Home Army pinned it hopes more than ever on help fror the outside. The Soviets refused t intervene, however, preferring t wait patiently on the east bank c the Vistula while the German crushed the insurgents. On Sep tember 7, the Poles opened surrer der negotiations with the Ninth Ar my, sending the president of th Polish Red Cross, Countess Tar nowska, to meet with senior Ge man officers. Three days later, Sc viet guns, silent for weeks, began thunder again. Assuming th meant that Russian help was on i way, the partisans abruptly ende the peace talks, and the Germar resumed their assault on the city

woman emerges to surrender to German troops. Partisans cut holes in walls to make courier routes.

wounded insurgent climbs from a sewer into the hands of waiting German soldiers.

A Time of Despair

The Soviets offered no help. Their artillery drove the German troops out of Warsaw's easternmost suburb and pushed them to the west bank of the Vistula. Then, the Soviet army settled down again to wait.

The German attacks in Warsaw, meanwhile, sent thousands to the city's makeshift hospitals, where a lack of medical supplies forced doctors to amputate limbs with handsaws and no anesthesia. Starving residents ate their pets, and when the Germans cut off the water supply, drank from puddles and licked damp basement walls.

American bombers that were attempting to relieve the plight of the city's citizens mistakenly parachuted supplies into German-held areas. To maintain a facade of support for the uprising, a few Soviet planes dropped ammunition—which did not fit the rebels' weapons. With no help in sight, Home Army leaders were compelled to reopen talks with the Germans.

Starving and exhausted Poles await their fate after climbing out of cellars and drainage pipes to surrender.

Clinging to their personal belongings, Poles line up for trains that will take them to concentration camps.

Laying Down Arms

On October 2 at 8:00 a.m., four representatives of the Polish Home Army met with SS General Erich von dem Bach-Zelewski, commander of the German forces in Warsaw. The insurgents agreed to capitulate if certain demands were met: All members of the Home Army were to be treated as prisoners of war according to international regulations; immunity would be granted to Home Army members sought for political crimes committed before the uprising; no reprisals would be taken against the Polish people.

After hours of haggling, the treaty was finally signed. More than 9,000 Home Army soldiers were sent to prisoner-of-war camps, but some 3,500 others went into hiding. The Germans crammed hundreds of thousands of weakened but still able-bodied Poles onto trains and shipped them to concentration camps. About 70,000 others, mostly women, children, the old, and the sick, were driven into the countryside and left to fend for themselves.

General Bor, head of the Home Army, surrenders to SS General Bach-Zelewsk

A soldier uses a flamethrower to torch the hideout of Home Army fighters who refused to surrender.

Annihilation of a City

The Germans reported 2,000 dead and 9,000 wounded in the sixty-three day uprising. About 16,000 partisans had perished or were missing and presumed to be dead. More than 200,000 civilians, almost one-fifth of Warsaw's population, died. Not content with this carnage, the Germans brought in demolition squads, who moved systematically through the city for the next three months and reduced museums, schools, theaters, hospitals, and private homes to little more than rubble and dust. Culturally and historically precious structures were not spared; Nazi architects and art historians led the wreckers to statues of Poland's heroes and to medieval churches and palaces to make certain that they would be destroyed. In one of his last addresses to the Reichstag, Hitler gloated, "Warsaw is now no more than a geographical term on the map of Europe."

Repaired and replaced on its column amid the debris of Castle Square in Old Town, a statue of King Sigismund III, seventeenth-century ruler of Poland, bears silent witness to the resilience of Warsaw. By war's end, 400,000 Poles had returned to the city and were living in the ruins.

Acknowledgments

The editors thank the following individuals and institutions for their help: Germany: Berlin—Heidi Klein, Bildarchiv Preussischer Kulturbesitz; Wolfgang Streubel, Ullstein Bilderdienst. Bielefeld—Hermann Ellersieg, Kock, Buch u. Offset Druck. Munich—Rüdiger von Manstein. Osnabrück—Karl-Walter Becker, Munin-Verlag. Rösrath-Hoffnungsthal—Helga Müller, Archiv Piekalkiewicz. Scheessel—Dr. Paul K. Schmidt-Carell. Stuttgart—Angelika Treiber, Bibliothek für Zeitgeschichte. Traben-Trarbach—Carl Henrich. Soviet Union: Moscow—Alexander M. Gusev and Victor A. Kyklenko, *The Soviet Soldier.* United States: Virginia—E. Andrew Cooke; Paul J. Gartenmann, Barcroft Books; Kevin Mahoney. Yugoslavia: Belgrade—Georgije Skrigin.

Picture Credits

Credits from left to right are separated by semicolons, from top to bottom by dashes. Cover: Bundesarchiv, Koblenz. 4-6: Süddeutscher Verlag Bilderdienst, Munich. 7: Agence Novosti, Paris. 8, 9: From *Verbrannte Erde* by Paul Carell, Ullstein, Frankfurt, 1985—Imperial War Museum, London; UPI/Bettmann, New York. 10: Süddeutscher Verlag Bilderdienst, Munich. 11: Bundesarchiv, Koblenz—courtesy John Calmann and King, London. 12, 13: From *The Soviet Soldier,* Moscow. 14: Archiv Dr. Paul K. Schmidt-Carell, Hamburg. 17: Map by R. R. Donnelley & Sons Company, Cartographic Services. 19-21: Ullstein Bilderdienst, Berlin. 22: From *Der Zweite Weltkrieg,* by Heinz Bergschicker, Pahl-Rugenstein, Cologne, 1952. 23: Bildarchiv Piekalkiewicz, Rösrath-Hoffnungsthal. 24, 25: Art by John Batchelor. 28, 29: Bundesarchiv, Koblenz. 30: Map by R. R. Donnelley & Sons Company, Cartographic Services. 33: Bundesarchiv, Koblenz. 34, 35: From *Wenn alle Brüder schweigen,* Munin-Verlag, Osnabrück, 1973; Bundesarchiv, Koblenz. 37: Süddeutscher Verlag Bilderdienst, Munich. 38: From *Wenn alle Brüder schweigen,* Munin-Verlag, Osnabrück, 1973. 40, 41: Archiv J. Piekalkiewicz, Rösrath-Hoffnungsthal. 42: From *Division Das Reich im Bild* by Otto Weidinger, Munin-Verlag, Osnabrück, 1981—Archiv J. Piekalkiewicz, Rösrath-Hoffnungsthal. 43: Bundesarchiv, Koblenz (5). 44: Mark Redkin. 45: Bundesarchiv, Koblenz. 46: Sovfoto, New York. 48: Archiv Dr. Paul K. Schmidt-Carell, Hamburg. 51: Bundesarchiv, Koblenz. 52, 53: National Archives 208-AH-32AJJ-15. 54, 55: Map by R. R. Donnelley & Sons Company, Cartographic Services. 57: The Hulton Picture Company, London. 58, 59: Bundesarchiv, Koblenz; courtesy Friedrich Trenz—Bundesarchiv, Koblenz; courtesy Friedrich Trenz. 61: National Archives 373. 63: Sovfoto, New York. 64, 65: From *The Soviet Soldier,* Moscow; Süddeutscher Verlag Bilderdienst, Munich. 66, 67: Imperial War Museum, London. 69: From *The Soviet Soldier,* Moscow. 70, 71: Ullstein Bilderdienst, Berlin. 72: From *Panzers in Russia* by Horst Scheibert and Ulrich Elfrath, Almark International, Podzun-Verlag, Dorheim, 1971. 73: From *The Soviet Soldier,* Moscow. 74, 75: National Archives 306-NT-12087-12. 77: Imperial War Museum, London. 78-89: Carl Henrich, Traben-Trarbach. 90: Archiv Dr. Paul K. Schmidt-Carell, Hamburg. 94, 95: From *The Great Fatherland War 1941-1945,* Vol. 4, Planeta, Moscow, 1979; Globe Photos, New York—The Hulton Picture Company, London. 96: E. Haldéi/Agence Novosti, Paris. 99: Map by R. R. Donnelley & Sons Company, Cartographic Services. 101: Ullstein Bilderdienst, Berlin. 102: From *The Great Fatherland War 1941-1945,* Vol. 3, Planeta, Moscow, 1987. 103: Bibliothek für Zeitgeschichte, Stuttgart—The Hulton Picture Company, London. 104: From *The Phantom War* by Matthew Cooper, Macdonald & Jane's, London, 1979 (2)—Archiv Gerstenberg, Wietze. 107: AP/Wide World, New York. 108, 109: Photo by Mark Redkin, from *The Russian War: 1941-1945,* edited by Daniela Mrazkova and Vladimir Remes, E. P. Dutton, New York, 1975. 111: Bibliothek für Zeitgeschichte, Stuttgart: Hoffmann Collection. 112: From *Wie ein Fels im Meer* by Karl Ullrich, Munin-Verlag, Osnabrück, 1984. 115-117: From *Der Zweite Weltkrieg* by Heinz Bergschicker, Pahl-Rugenstein, Cologne, 1952. 118: Dmitri Baltermants, Moscow. 119: From *The Soviet Soldier,* Moscow. 120: The National Archives 208-AA-330D-1. 122: Map by R. R. Donnelley & Sons Company, Cartographic Services. 123: Bundesarchiv, Koblenz. 124: UPI/Bettmann, New York. 125: Bundesarchiv, Koblenz. 126, 127: From *SS Gebirgs-Division Prinz Eugen im Bild* by Otto Kumm, Munin-Verlag, Osnabrück, 1983—Bundesarchiv, Koblenz; UPI/Bettmann, New York. 128, 129: Georgije Skrigin, Belgrade. 130, 131: Bettmann, New York. 132: Ullstein Bilderdienst, Berlin. 135: From *Verrantene Schlachten* by Hans Friessner, Holsten-Verlag, Hamburg, 1956. 137: Map by R. R. Donnelley & Sons Company, Cartographic Services. 139: National Archives 208-N-27953FA. 142: From *L'Armée Allemande en URSS en images,* courtesy Éditions Libro-Sciences. 144, 145: National Archives 208-AA-330FF2. 146, 147: The Hulton Picture Company, London. 149-151: Süddeutscher Verlag Bilderdienst, Munich. 153: From *A Picture of the Second World War* by Ölvedi Ignác, Europa Könyviadó, 1969. 154, 155: Ullstein Bilderdienst, Berlin; Archives Tallandier, Paris. 156, 157: Bundesarchiv, Koblenz. 159: From *Verrantene Schlachten* by Hans Friessner, Holsten-Verlag, Hamburg, 1956. 161: From *A Picture of the Second World War* by Ölvedi Ignác, Europa Könyviadó, 1969. 162, 163: Ullstein Bilderdienst, Berlin. 164, 165: Robert Hunt Library, London; UPI/Bettmann, New York. 166: Muzeum Historyczne, Warsaw; UPI/Bettmann, New York—The Hulton Picture Company, London. 167: Muzeum Historyczne, Warsaw. 168: Ullstein Bilderdienst, Berlin. 169: Bundesarchiv, Koblenz—Presseillustrationen Heinrich R. Hoffmann, Munich. 170, 171: Sylvester Kris-Braun, Muzeum Historyczne, Warsaw; UPI/Bettmann, New York. 172, 173: Ullstein Bilderdienst, Berlin—from *2194 Days of War,* compiled by Cesare Salmaggi and Alfredo Pallavisini, Gallery Books, New York, 1979; The Hulton Picture Company, London. 174, 175: Wide World Photos, New York; Süddeutscher Verlag Bilderdienst, Munich—Ullstein Bilderdienst, Berlin. 176, 177: UPI/Bettmann, New York.

Bibliography

Books

Angolia, John R., and Adolf Schlicht, *Uniforms & Traditions of the German Army, 1933-1945.* San Jose, Calif.: R. James Bender, 1987.

Armstrong, John Alexander, ed., *Soviet Partisans in World War II.* Madison: University of Wisconsin Press, 1964.

Bielecki, Tadeusz, and Leszek Szymanski, *Warsaw Aflame: The 1939-1945 Years.* Los Angeles: Polamerica Press, 1973.

Blunden, Godfrey, and the Editors of Time-Life Books, *Eastern Europe: Czechoslovakia, Hungary, Poland* (Life World Library series). New York: Time-Life Books, 1965.

Bruce, George, *The Warsaw Uprising.* London: Pan Books, 1972.

Buell, Thomas B., et al., *The Second World War.* Wayne, N.J.: Avery, 1984.

Carell, Paul, *Scorched Earth.* Transl. by Ewald Osers. Boston: Little, Brown, 1970.

Clark, Alan, *Barbarossa.* New York: Quill, 1965.

Cooper, Matthew, *The Nazi War against Soviet Partisans, 1941-1944.* New York: Stein and Day, 1979.

Darby, H. C., et al., *A Short History of Yugoslavia: From Early Times to 1966.* Ed. by Stephen Clissold. Cambridge: Cambridge University Press, 1968.

Davies, W. J. K., *German Army Handbook, 1939-1945.* New York: Arco, 1973.

Dedijer, Vladimir, *With Tito through the War.* London: Alexander Hamilton, 1951.

Deschner, Gunther, *Warsaw Rising.* New York: Ballantine Books, 1972.

Djilas, Milovan, *Wartime.* Transl. by Michael B. Petrovich. New York: Harcourt Brace Jovanovich, 1977.

Donlagić, Ahmet, Žarko Atanacković, and Dušan Plenča, *Yugoslavia in the Second World War.* Transl. by Lovett F. Edwards. Belgrade: Medunarodna Stampa—Interpress, 1967.

Drozdov, Georgii, and Evgenii Ryabko, *Russia at War, 1941-1945.* Ed. by Carey Schofield, transl. by Lydia Kmetyuk. New York: Vendome Press, 1987.

Drum, Karl, *Airpower and Russian Partisan Warfare.* Ed. by Littleton B. Atkinson. USAF Historical Studies: no. 177. New York: Arno Press, 1962.

Dupuy, T. N., and Paul Martell, *Great Battles on the Eastern Front.* New York: Bobbs-Merrill, 1982.

Erickson, John, *The Road to Berlin.* Boulder, Colo.: Westview Press, 1983.

Fey, Will, *Armor Battles of the Waffen-SS, 1943-1945.* Transl. by Harri Henschler. Manitoba, Canada: J. J. Fedorowicz, 1990.

Friessner, Hans, *Verratene Schlachten.* Hamburg, Germany: Holsten-Verlag Schenke & Hass, 1956.

Guderian, Heinz, *Panzer Leader.* Transl. by Constantine FitzGibbon. London: Michael Joseph, 1952.

Hæstrup, Jørgen, *Europe Ablaze.* Odense, Denmark: Odense University Press, 1978.

Homze, Edward L., *Foreign Labor in Nazi Germany.* Princeton, N.J.: Princeton University Press, 1967.

Hoptner, Jacob B., *Yugoslavia in Crisis, 1934-1941.* New York: Columbia University Press, 1962.

Hoyt, Edwin P., *Hitler's War.* New York: McGraw-Hill, 1988.

Icks, Robert J., *Tanks and Armored Vehicles, 1900-1945.* Ed. by Phillip Andrews. Old Greenwich, Conn.: WE, Inc., n.d.

Jarrett, George B., *Combat Tanks.* New York: Meredith Press, 1969.

Jukes, Geoffrey, *Kursk: The Clash of Armour.* New York: Ballantine Books, 1968.

Kulski, Julian Eugeniusz, *Dying, We Live.* New York: Holt, Rinehart and Winston, 1979.

Kumm, Otto, *7. SS-Gebirgs-Division "Prinz Eugen" im Bild.* Osnabrück, Germany: Munin-Verlag, 1983.

Littlejohn, David, *Foreign Legions of the Third Reich* (Vol. 3). San Jose, Calif.: R. James Bender, 1985.

Maclean, Fitzroy, *Tito: A Pictorial Biography.* New York: McGraw-Hill, 1980.

Madej, W. Victor:
The Russo-German War: Autumn 1944-25 January 1945. Allentown, Pa.: Valor, 1987.
The Russo-German War: Balkans, November 1940 to November 1944. Allentown, Pa.: Valor, 1990.
The Russo-German War: Summer-Autumn 1943. Allentown, Pa.: Valor, 1987.
The Russo-German War: Winter and Spring 1944: Battles for Central Europe. Allentown, Pa.: Valor, 1988.

Madej, W. Victor, ed., *German Army Order of Battle.* Allentown, Pa.: Game, 1985.

Manstein, Erich von, *Lost Victories.* Ed. and transl. by Anthony G. Powell. Chicago: Henry Regnery, 1958.

Mellenthin, Friedrich W. von:
German Generals of World War II: As I Saw Them. Norman: University of Oklahoma Press, 1977.
Panzer Battles: A Study of the Employment of Armor in the Second World War. Ed. by L. C. F. Turner, transl. by H. Betzler. Norman: University of Oklahoma Press, 1956.

Milazzo, Matteo J., *The Chetnik Movement & the Yugoslav Resistance.* Baltimore: Johns Hopkins University Press, 1975.

Mountfield, David, *The Partisans.* London: Hamlyn, 1979.

Niepold, Gerd, *Battle for White Russia: The Destruction of Army Group Centre, June 1944.* Transl. by Richard Simpkin. London: Brassey's Defence, 1987.

Palmer, Alan, *The Lands Between: A History of East-Central Europe since the Congress of Vienna.* New York: Macmillan, 1970.

Perrett, Bryan:
The PzKpfw V Panther. London: Osprey, 1981.
The Tiger Tanks. London: Osprey, 1981.

Piekalkiewicz, Janusz, *Operation "Citadel": Kursk and Orel: The Greatest Tank Battle of the Second World War.* Transl. by Michaela Nierhaus. Novato, Calif.: Presidio Press, 1987.

Roberts, Walter R., *Tito, Mihailović, and the Allies, 1941-1945.* New Brunswick, N.J.: Rutgers University Press, 1973.

Scheibert, Horst, *The Panther Family.* Transl. by Edward Force. West Chester, Pa.: Schiffer, 1990.

Seaton, Albert, *The Russo-German War, 1941-45.* New York: Praeger, 1970.

Senger und Etterlin, F. M. von, *German Tanks of World War II.* Ed. by Peter Chamberlain and Chris Ellis, transl. by J. Lucas. Harrisburg, Pa.: Stackpole Books, 1969.

Shores, Christopher, *Duel for the Sky.* Garden City, N.Y.: Doubleday, 1985.

Skorzeny, Otto, *Skorzeny's Special Missions.* London: Robert Hale, 1957.

Tomasevich, Jozo, *The Chetniks.* Stanford, Calif.: Stanford University Press, 1975.

Werth, Alexander, *Russia at War: 1941-1945.* New York: Carroll & Graf, 1964.

White, B. T., *German Tanks & Armored Vehicles, 1914-1945.* New York: Arco, 1968.

Whiting, Charles, *Skorzeny.* New York: Ballantine Books, 1972.

Wolff, Robert Lee, *The Balkans in Our Time.* Cambridge, Mass.: Harvard University Press, 1956.

Zawodny, J. K., *Nothing but Honour.* London: Macmillan, 1978.

Ziemke, Earl F., *Stalingrad to Berlin.* Washington, D.C.: Office of the Chief of Military History, United States Army, 1968.

Zins, Alfred, *Die Operation Zitadelle.* Frankfurt am Main, Germany: Peter Lang, 1986.

Other Publications

"The German Campaigns in the Balkans (Spring 1941)." Department of the Army Pamphlet 20-260. Washington, D.C.: Department of the Army, 1953.

Howell, Edgar M., "The Soviet Partisan Movement, 1941-1944." Department of the Army Pamphlet 20-244. Washington, D.C.: Department of the Army, 1956.

Pallud, Jean Paul, "Budapest." *After the Battle,* no. 40.

Index

Numerals in italics indicate an illustration of the subject mentioned.